Moving West Songbook

with historical commentary

Compiled and edited by Keith & Rusty McNeil

Companion to the recording
Moving West Songs with historical narration

WEM Records
Riverside, California

Songbooks and recordings by Keith & Rusty McNeil

Songbooks

Colonial & Revolution Songbook with historical commentary
Civil War Songbook with historical commentary
California Songbook with historical commentary
Moving West Songbook with historical commentary

Recordings

American History Through Folksong

Colonial & Revolution Songs with historical narration
Moving West Songs with historical narration
Civil War Songs with historical narration
Cowboy Songs with historical narration
Western Railroad Songs with historical narration
Working & Union Songs with historical narration

California History Through Folksong

California Songs with historical narration - Volume One 19th Century
California Songs with historical narration - Volume Two 20th Century

Singing the Holiday Season

Folksongs for Children

Coarse & Fine

ISBN 1-878360-30-2

Copyright, © 2003, by WEM Records
a division of McNeil Music, Inc.
16230 Van Buren Boulevard
Riverside, California 92504
www.wemrecords.com

Contents

Territorial Expansion and Abolition

Texas and the Mexican War

Minstrel Shows and the California Gold Rush

Immigrants from China, Ireland and Germany

Introduction

In 1803, President Thomas Jefferson's acquisition of the Louisiana Territory from France doubled the size of the United States.

In 1804, Meriwether Lewis and his friend William Clark set out on their two and a half year expedition to explore the Louisiana Territory from St. Louis, Missouri to the mouth of the Columbia River at the Pacific Ocean.

In 1811, John Jacob Astor's fur company founded Astoria in what is now Oregon.

In 1815, the War of 1812 ended with the ratification of the Treaty of Ghent. The United States' relations with Great Britain improved quickly after the war's end.

In 1819, Spain sold East and West Florida to the United States, and Russia ceded its claim south of 54° 40' to Great Britain and the United States.

In 1836, Texas became an independent republic.

In 1845, Texas became a part of the United States.

In 1846, the United States settled the Oregon boundary dispute with Britain.

In 1848, Mexico ceded to the United States what is now California, Arizona, Nevada and Utah, along with parts of Wyoming, Colorado and New Mexico.

In 1851, John Soule, an Indiana newspaperman, coined the phrase "Go West, young man." *New York Tribune* founder and editor Horace Greeley popularized the phrase.

As the new nation expanded, large numbers of America's citizens and immigrants moved West.

Monticello, Jefferson's home

Forward

America's songs reflect the attitudes, sorrows, joys, fears, humor, religions, politics and occupations of its citizens. Immigrants brought songs from the Old Country and wrote songs in the New World. Americans also wrote new words to old songs, foreign and home grown.[1] This book gives a sampling of some of the songs that flavored the American story as the nation expanded during the half-century following the War of 1812. As people moved westward, they wrote dozens of new songs using old tunes. The evolution of "Old Rosin the Beau," one of 19th century America's favorite songs, is a typical example of the American folk music process.

This popular Irish drinking song first appeared in print in America in 1838 and became a popular American drinking song. Here are the words from the original Irish version.

[1] For example, the old camp meeting song "Say Brothers Will You Meet Us" became "The Battle Hymn of the Republic," "John Brown's Body," "Hang Jeff Davis in the Sour Apple Tree," and countless others over the past hundred and fifty years. The old gospel hymn "Hallelujah Thine the Glory" became the hobo song "Hallelujah I'm A Bum," which in turn became the 1960s' freedom riders' song "Hallelujah I'm A-travellin'."

Old Rosin the Beau

Words and Music: Anonymous.

I live for the good of my na-tion, and my sons are all grow-ing low, But I hope that the next gen-er-a-tion will re-sem-ble Old Ros-in, the Beau.

Chorus

Will re-sem-ble Old Ros-in, the Beau, re-sem-ble Old Ros-in, the Beau, I hope that the next gen-er-a-tion will re-sem-ble Old Ros-in, the Beau.

I live for the good of my nation, and my sons are all growing low,
But I hope that the next generation will resemble Old Rosin, the Beau.
    Will resemble Old Rosin, the Beau, resemble Old Rosin, the Beau,
    I hope that the next generation will resemble Old Rosin, the Beau.

I've traveled this country all over, and now to the next I will go,
For I know that good quarters await me to welcome Old Rosin, the Beau.
    To welcome Old Rosin, the Beau, to welcome Old Rosin, the Beau,
    I know that good quarters await me to welcome Old Rosin, the Beau.

In the gay round of pleasure I've traveled, nor will I behind leave a foe,
And when my companions are jovial they'll drink to Old Rosin, the Beau.
    They'll drink to Old Rosin, the Beau,....etc.

But now my life's drawn to a closing, and all will at last be so,
So we'll take a full bumper at parting, to the name of Old Rosin, the Beau.

When I'm dead and laid out on the counter, the people all making a show,
Just sprinkle plain whiskey and water on the corpse of Old Rosin, the Beau.

Then get a full dozen young fellows and stand them all 'round in a row,
And drink out of half-gallon bottles to the name of Old Rosin, the Beau.

Then get four or five jovial fellows, and let them all staggering go,
And dig a bog hole in the meadow, and in it toss Rosin, the Beau.

Then get you a couple of tombstones, put one at my head and my toe,
And do not forget to scratch on them the good name of Old Rosin, the Beau.

I feel that grim tyrant approaching, the cruel impeccable old foe,
That spares neither age nor condition, not even Old Rosin, the Beau.

In 1838, shortly after "Old Rosin the Beau" arrived in Harrisburg, Pennsylvania, the Washington Temperance Society of Harrisburg turned the drinking song into a temperance song called "The Washington Badge."

The Washington Badge

Words and Music: Anonymous.

Come join in our temperance army, and put on the Washington badge,
I'm sure that it never will harm you to give in your name to the pledge.
        To give in your name to the pledge, to give in your name to the pledge,
        I'm sure that it never will harm you to give in your name to the pledge.

We've done with our days of carousing, our nights, too, of frolicsome glee,
For now with our sober minds choosing, we've pledged ourselves never to spree.
        We've pledged ourselves never to spree, we've pledged ourselves never to spree,
        For now with our sober minds choosing, we've pledged ourselves never to spree.

The "Old Rosin" melody became the white spiritual "Sawyer's Exit" as people moved southwest into Louisiana and Mississippi in the decades following the War of 1812. According to legend, Reverend S. B. Sawyer wrote the words to the song "Sawyer's Exit" the day he died, with instructions that it should be sung to "Old Rosin the Beau." John Massengale arranged the song in shape note format, and it was published in the *Sacred Harp*, a popular 19th century southern shape note hymnal. The shape notes were so called because each note of the scale had its own shape. Instead of "do, re, mi, fa, sol, la, ti, do," people sang, "fa, sol, la, fa, sol, la, mi, fa." Fa was a triangle, sol a circle, la a square and mi a diamond. Shape note singers in the southern United States traditionally stood in a hollow square (treble, tenor and bass), sang the syllables first, and then sang the words.

Sawyer's Exit

Words: S. B. Sawyer. Music: Anonymous.

How bright is the day when the Christian, Receives the sweet mes-sage to come, To rise to the man-sions of
glo-ry, And be there for-ev-er at home, And

be there for-ev-er at home, And be there for-ev-er at

home, To rise to the man-sions of glo-ry, And

be there for-ev-er at home.

How bright is the day when the Christian,
Receives the sweet message to come,
To rise to the mansions of glory,
And be there forever at home.

CHORUS
And be there forever at home,
And be there forever at home,
To rise to the mansions of glory,
And be there forever at home.

The angels stand ready and waiting,
The moment the spirit is gone,
To carry it upward to heaven,
And welcome it safely at home.

CHORUS
And welcome it safely at home,
And welcome it safely at home,
To carry it upward to heaven,
And welcome it safely at home.

The saints that have gone up before us,
All raise a new shout as we come,
And sing hallelujah the louder,
To welcome the travelers home. CHORUS

And there are our friends and companions,
Escaped from the evil to come,
And crowding the gates of fair Zion
To wait our arrival at home. CHORUS

And there is the blessed Redeemer,
So mild in his merciful throne,
With hearts and hands widely extended
To welcome his ransomed ones home. CHORUS

Then let us go onward rejoicing,
Till Jesus invites us to come,
To share in his glorious kingdom,
And rest in his bosom at home. CHORUS

While "Sawyer's Exit" was popular among shape note singers in the South, Midwestern Republicans were using the tune for Abraham Lincoln's famous campaign song "Lincoln and Liberty."

Lincoln and Liberty

Words: F. A. Simkins. Music: Anonymous.

Hurrah to the choice of the nation, our chieftain so brave and so true,
We'll go for the great reformation, for Lincoln and Liberty, too.
We'll go for the son of Kentucky, the hero of Hoosierdom through,
The Pride of the Suckers, so lucky, for Lincoln and Liberty, too.

They'll find what by felling and mauling, our rail-maker statesman can do,
For the people are everywhere calling for Lincoln and Liberty, too.
Then up with the banner so glorious, the star-spangled red, white and blue,
We'll fight till our banner's victorious for Lincoln and Liberty, too.

Our David's good sling is unerring, the Slavocrat's giant he slew,
Then shout for the freedom preferring for Lincoln and Liberty, too.
We'll go for the son of Kentucky, the hero of Hoosierdom through,
The pride of the Suckers, so lucky, for Lincoln and Liberty, too.

The tune for "Old Rosin the Beau" was taken up by populist farmers on the plains and in California when it became "Hayseed Like Me." The words were published in the *Farmer's Alliance* in 1890.

Hayseed Like Me

Words: Arthur L. Kellogg. Music: Anonymous.

I once was a tool of oppression, as green as a sucker could be,
When monopolies banded together, to beat a poor hayseed like me.
To beat a poor hayseed like me, to beat a poor hayseed like me,
When monopolies banded together, to beat a poor hayseed like me.

The railroads and old party bosses, together did sweetly agree,
They thought there would be little trouble, in working a hayseed like me.
In working a hayseed like me, in working a hayseed like me,
They thought there would be little trouble, in working a hayseed like me.

But now I've roused up a little, their greed and corruption I see,
And the ticket we vote next November will be made up of hayseeds like me!
Will be made up of hayseeds like me! Will be made up of hayseeds like me!
And the ticket we vote next November will be made up of hayseeds like me!

"Old Rosin's" tune also made its way to the Puget Sound in the Pacific Northwest, when Judge Francis B. Henry's song "The Old Settler" was published in 1874. The song is also known as "The Old Settler's Song" and "Acres of Clams."[2]

The Old Settler

Words: Francis B. Henry. Music: Anonymous.

I've traveled all over this country, prospecting and looking for gold,
I've tunneled, hydraulicked and cradled, and I have been frequently sold.

CHORUS
And I have been frequently sold, and I have been frequently sold,
I've tunneled, hydraulicked and cradled, and I have been frequently sold.

For one who gets riches by mining, perceiving that hundreds grow poor,
I made up my mind to try farming, the only pursuit that is sure.

CHORUS
The only pursuit that is sure, the only pursuit that is sure,
I made up my mind to try farming, the only pursuit that is sure.

So rolling my grub in my blanket, I left all my tools on the ground,
And started one morning to shank it, for the country they call Puget Sound. CHORUS

Arriving flat broke in mid-winter, I found it enveloped in fog,
And covered all over with timber, thick as hair on the back of a dog. CHORUS

As I looked on the prospect so gloomy the tears trickled over my face,
For I felt that my travels had brought me to the edge of the jumping-off place. CHORUS

I took up a claim in the forest, and sat myself down to hard toil,
For two years I chopped and I niggard, but never got down to the soil. CHORUS

I tried to get out of the country, but poverty forced me to stay,
Until I became an Old Settler, then nothing could drive me away. CHORUS

And now that I'm used to the climate, I think that if man ever found
A spot to live easy and happy, that Eden is on Puget Sound. CHORUS

No longer the slave of ambition, I laugh at the world and its shams,
As I think of my pleasant condition, surrounded by acres of clams! CHORUS

[2] According to British folklorist Peter Kennedy, in his book *Folksongs of Britain and Ireland*, the tune has continued to remain popular in Ireland and Britain, not only as a song, but also as a jig tune for quadrilles and country dances, and, slowly, as a waltz.

Territorial Expansion and Abolition

To the West

The first half of the nineteenth century saw some radical changes in America: geographical, political, social and ethnic. These changes involved huge territorial expansion and exploration, and the great migration of people into the Northwest Territory, the Mississippi Valley, the Southwest, the Salt Lake Valley, Oregon and California.

In the first two decades of the 1800s, with the Louisiana Purchase and the acquisition of Florida, the United States more than doubled its territory, adding about 860,000 square miles. As Americans looked westward, two major inland waterways beckoned: the Mississippi River and its tributaries, and the Great Lakes. The Mississippi River system provided about 14,000 miles of navigable waterways, spanning the huge territory between the Appalachian Mountains in the East and the Rocky Mountains in the West.

The opportunities staggered the imaginations of Americans and Europeans. Scotsman Charles McKay never came to the United States, but his song "To the West" did, and became popular in America.

Horace Greeley

To the West

Words: Charles McKay. Music: Henry Russell.

To the West! to the West! to the land of the free, Where might-y Mis-sour-i rolls down to the sea, Where a man is a man, if he's wil-ling to toil, And the hum-blest may gath-er the fruits of the soil. Where chil-dren are bless-ings, and he who hath

most, Has aid for his for-tune and rich-es to

boast, Where the young may ex-ult, and the a-ged may

rest, A - way far a - way, to the land of the

chorus
West! To the West! to the West! to the land of the

free, Where might-y Mis-sour-i rolls down to the

sea, Where the young may ex-ult and the a-ged may

rest, A - way far a - way, to the land of the West!

To the West! to the West! to the land of the free,
Where the mighty Missouri rolls down to the sea,
Where a man is a man, if he's willing to toil,
And the humblest may gather the fruits of the soil.
Where children are blessings, and he who hath most,
Has aid for his fortune and riches to boast,
Where the young may exult, and the aged may rest,
Away far away, to the land of the West!
To the West! to the West! to the land of the free,
Where the mighty Missouri rolls down to the sea,
Where the young may exult and the aged may rest,
Away far away, to the land of the West!

To the West! to the West! where the rivers that flow,
Run thousands of miles, spreading out as they go,
Where the green waving forests shall echo our call,
As wide as all England, and free to us all!
Where the prairies like seas, where the billows have rolled,
Are broad as the kingdoms and empires of old,

And the lakes are like oceans, in storm or in rest,
Away, far away, to the land of the West!
To the West! to the West! where the rivers that flow,
Run thousands of miles, spreading out as they go,
Where the green waving forests shall echo our call,
As wide as all England, and free to us all!

To the West! to the West! there is wealth to be won,
The forest to clear is the work to be done,
Where the stars and the stripes, like a banner unfurled,
Invites to its regions the world, all the world.
Where the people are true to the vows that they frame,
And their pride is the honor that's shown to their name.
Away, far away, let us hope for the best,
And build up a home in the land of the West!
To the West! to the West! there is wealth to be won,
The forest to clear is the work to be done,
Where the stars and the stripes, like a banner unfurled,
Invites to its regions the world, all the world!

In the 1850s, J. E. Johnson parodied McKay's song and published it in his gold rush song book *Johnson's Original Comic Songs*:

To the West, to the West, I once went, do you see,
And one visit I'm sure was sufficient for me,
Oh the things that I saw there they frightened me quite,
And ever since then sirs, I've scarcely been right.
My children got sick every day, sirs, almost,
And my wife took the chills and got deaf as a post,
Oh there's some may exult, but for me, sirs, I'm blest
If I haven't had as much as I want of the West!

The Erie Canal

The Erie Canal

The Great Lakes provided natural waterways for the Northwest Territory, which included Ohio, Indiana, Illinois, Michigan, Wisconsin and Minnesota. Migration to the Northwest Territory began immediately after the American Revolution, increasing the non-Indian population from 100,000 to 400,000 between 1790 and 1800. After the War of 1812 the New York state legislature proposed the building of a canal from Albany to Buffalo, which would connect the Great Lakes system with the Atlantic Ocean.

Construction began on the Erie Canal in 1817, and the last section was completed in 1825. The canal stimulated tremendous growth in the Northwest Territory. It was so successful that by 1847 the canal business at Albany was greater than New Orleans received from the entire Mississippi system.

Most of the many ballads written about the Erie Canal were tongue-in-cheek, about the "dangers" of the "raging" canal. The bargemen weren't sailors, they led the mules or horses along the towpath. The work was boring, and at night the towpath boys sang to keep themselves awake and to while away the hours. Singing was so common that residents who lived near the canal sometimes complained to the authorities about the night-singers.

The Erie Canal

Words and Music: Anonymous.

We were for-ty miles from Al-ba-ny, For-get it I nev-er shall. What a ter-ri-ble storm we had one night On the E-ri-e Ca-nal. Oh the E-ri-e was a-ris-in', And the gin was get-tin' low. And I scarce-ly think we'll get a drink till we get to Buf-fa-lo, Till we get to Buf-fa-lo.

We were forty miles from Albany,
Forget it I never shall.
What a terrible storm we had one night
On the Er-i-e Canal.

CHORUS
Oh, the Er-i-e was a risin',
And the gin was gettin' low.
And I scarcely think we'll get a drink
    till we get to Buffalo,
Till we get to Buffalo.

Our cook she was a grand old gal,
She wore a ragged dress,
We heisted her upon the mast
As a signal of distress. CHORUS

We were loaded down with barley,
We were chock up full of rye.
And the captain he looked down at me
With his goddam wicked eye! CHORUS

Two days out from Syracuse
The vessel struck a shoal,
We like to all been foundered
On a chunk of Lackawanna coal.
CHORUS

We hollered to the captain
On the towpath treadin' dirt,
He jumped on board and stopped the leak
With his old red flannel shirt. CHORUS

The winds began to whistle,
And the waves began to roll.
We had to reef our royals
On the raging canal. CHORUS

When we arrived at Buffalo,
With Sally, Jack and Hank,
We greased ourselves in tallow fat
And slid off on the plank! CHORUS

Now Sally's in the poorhouse.
The crew is all in jail.
I'm the only livin' sea cook's son
That's left to tell the tale. CHORUS

The Wisconsin Emigrant

   Despite the large migration to the Northwest Territory, there were many who resisted this temptation and chose to remain in New England. "The Wisconsin Emigrant" tells the story of one of the many families who stayed behind.

New England settlers

   "The Wisconsin Emigrant" eventually found its way to the Ozarks, where the wife convinces her husband to stay on his farm and not go to California.

The Wisconsin Emigrant

Words and Music: Anonymous.

Since times are so hard, I've thought my true heart, Of leav - ing my ox - en, my plow and my cart, And a - way to Wis - con - sin a jour - ney we'd go, To dou - ble our for - tune as oth - er folks do. While here I must la - bor each day in the field, And the win - ter con - sumes all the - sum - mer doth yield.

Since times are so hard, I've thought my true heart,
Of leaving my oxen, my plow and my cart,
And away to Wisconsin a journey we'd go,
To double our fortune as other folks do.
While here I must labor each day in the field,
And the winter consumes all the summer doth yield.

Oh husband I've noticed, with sorrowful heart,
You've neglected your oxen, your plow and your cart,
Your sheep are disordered, at random they run,
And your new Sunday suit is now every day on.
Oh stay on the farm and you'll suffer no loss,
For the stone that keeps rollin' will gather no moss.

Oh wife let's go, don't let us wait,
I long to be there, I long to be great,
You'll be a rich lady, and who knows but I
Some governor may be before that I die.
While here I must labor each day in the field,
And the winter consumes all the summer doth yield.

Oh husband remember that land must be cleared,
Which will cost you the labor of many a year.
Where horses, sheep, cattle and hogs are to buy,
And you'll scarcely get settled before you must die.
Oh stay on the farm and you'll suffer no loss,
For the stone that keeps rollin' will gather no moss.

Oh wife, let's go, don't let us stay,
I'll buy me a farm that is cleared by the way,
Where horses, sheep, cattle and hogs are not dear,
And we'll feast on fat buffalo half of the year.
While here I must labor each day in the field,
And the winter consumes all the summer doth yield.

Oh husband remember that land of delight,
Is surrounded by Indians who murder by night.
Your house they will plunder and burn to the ground,
While your wife and your children lie murdered around.
Oh stay on the farm and you'll suffer no loss,
For the stone that keeps rollin' will gather no moss.

Now wife you've convinced me, I'll argue no more,
I never had thought of your dyin' before.
I love my dear children although they are small,
But you, my dear wife, are more precious than all.
We'll stay on the farm and we'll suffer no loss,
For the stone that keeps rollin' will gather no moss.
Yes, we'll stay on the farm and we'll suffer no loss,
For the stone that keeps rollin' will gather no moss.

The Shanty-Man's Life

Logging was one of the earliest of the Lake State industries. The lumberjacks lived in flimsy shanties, and were called "shanty-men." With their colorful clothing, swaggering behavior and dangerous occupation, the lumberjacks became folk heroes, and many a farmer's daughter fell under the spell of the shanty-man.

The Shanty-Man's Life

Words and Music: Anonymous.

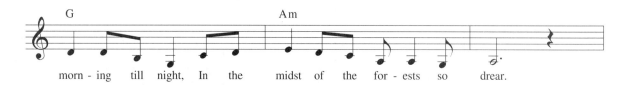

Oh a shanty-man's life is a wearisome life,
Although some think it void of care,
Swinging an ax from morning till night,
In the midst of the forests so drear.
Lying in the shanty bleak and cold,
While the cold stormy wintry winds blow,
And as soon as the daylight doth appear,
To the wild woods they must go.

Oh the cook rises up in the middle of the night
Saying, "Hurrah brave boys it is day."
Broken slumbers oft-times are past
As the cold winter night whiles away.
Had they rum, wine or beer their spirits for to cheer,
As the days so lonely do dwine,
Or a glass of any shone while in the woods alone,
For to cheer up their troubled minds.

But when spring it does set in double hardships then begin,
When the waters are piercing cold,
And their clothes are dripping wet and fingers benumbed
And their pike poles they scarcely can hold.
Betwixt rocks, shoals and sands give employment to all hands,
Their well-banded raft for to steer,
And the rapids that they run, oh they seem to them but fun,
For they're void of all slavish fear.

Oh a shanty lad is the only lad I love,
And I never will deny the same.
My heart does scorn these conceited farmer boys
Who think it a disgraceful name,
They may boast about their farms but my shanty-boy has charms
So far, far surpassing them all,
Until death it doth us part he shall enjoy my heart,
Let his riches be great or small.

Shantymen

The Jam on Gerry's Rocks

Logging was one of the most dangerous of all the frontier occupations. Rivermen would ride the logs on narrow, swift streams for two or three weeks with a minimum of sleep. The rapids and waterfalls were dangerous, and the log jams even more so. When a few logs became caught, the logs behind piled up. The only way to free the jam was to locate the key log and pry it loose, releasing the pile of logs and a wall of water. The rivermen ran across the logs to safety. If a man slipped, he was killed.

The best loved of all the shanty-boy songs was "The Jam on Gerry's Rocks." The "deacon seat" was a seat or board running along the wall of the bunkhouse between the lower bunks. The shanty-men sat on the deacon seat to drink, swap songs and tell stories.

According to folk music scholar Alan Lomax, folklorists attempted for many years to locate Gerry's Rocks, searching throughout the northeastern United States and in the Canadian Maritime provinces, to no avail.

The Jam on Gerry's Rocks

Words and Music: Anonymous.

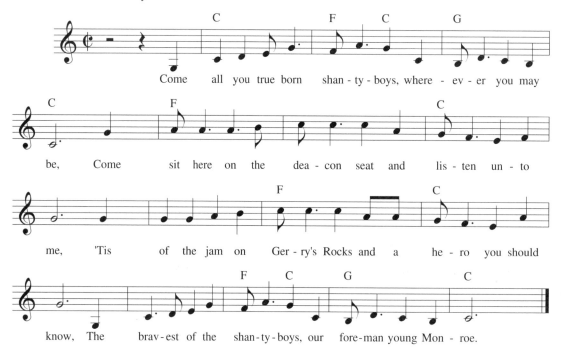

Come all you true born shanty-boys, wherever you may be,
Come sit here on the deacon seat and listen unto me,
'Tis of the jam on Gerry's Rocks and a hero you should know,
The bravest of the shanty-boys, our foreman young Monroe.

'Twas on a Sunday morning, ere daylight did appear,
The logs were piled up mountain high, we could not keep 'em clear,
Till six of our brave shanty-boys did volunteer to go,
And break the jam on Gerry's Rocks with foreman young Monroe.

They had not picked off many a log ere Monroe he did say,
"I'll send you off the drive, boys, for the jam will soon give way."
Alone he freed the key log, and then the jam did go,
It carried away on the boiling flood our foreman young Monroe.

Now when the boys up at the camp the sad news came to hear,
In search of his dead body down the river they did steer,
And there they found to their surprise, and sorrow, grief and woe,
All cut and mangled on the beach lay the form of young Monroe.

They picked him up most tenderly, smoothed back his raven hair.
There was one among the watchers whose cries did rend the air,
The fairest lass of Saginaw let tears of anguish flow,
But her moans and cries could not awake her true love young Monroe.

The Missus Clark, a widow, lived by the riverside,
This was her only daughter, Monroe's intended bride.
So the wages of her perished love the boss to her did pay
And a gift of gold was sent to her by the shanty-boys next day.

When she received the money, she thanked them tearfully,
But it was not her portion long on this world to be,
For it was just six weeks or so when she was called to go,
And the shanty-boys laid her at rest by the side of young Monroe.

They decked the graves most decently, 'twas on the fourth of May,
Come all ye true-born shanty-boys and for a comrade pray.
Engraven on a hemlock tree which by the beach did grow,
Are the name and date of the mournful fate of the foreman, young Monroe.

Log jam

Shenandoah

While settlers were moving into the Great Lakes areas, the mountain men and French-Canadian voyageurs were exploring the West and the Pacific Northwest in search of beaver. Outfitted in St. Louis, the mountain men, who later became the guides for the wagon trains, pushed up the Missouri River, trapping and exploring the mountain ranges from the Rockies to the Sierras, and from the Columbia River to the Mojave Desert. They traded, fought and lived with the Indians. They trapped in the fall and spring, sold their beaver pelts at the summer rendezvous, and then re-outfitted for the coming season.

One of America's favorite songs, "Shenandoah," is believed to have originated among the fur traders in the upper Missouri River area. It eventually found its way to sea and became a favorite capstan chantey among both American and British sailors. The song was sung while turning the capstan to raise the anchor, often within earshot of wives and sweethearts. As a result, "Shenandoah" remained one of the few sea chanteys devoid of profanity and bawdy language.[3]

Shenandoah

Words and Music: Anonymous.

Oh Shen - an - doah I long to see you,
A - - - way you rol - ling riv - er,
Oh Shen - an - doah I long to see you,
A - way we're bound a - way
'Cross the wide Mis - sour - i.

[3] The American cavalry on the western plains sang their own versions of "Shenandoah." Those versions were far from genteel.

Oh Shenandoah I long to see you,
Away you rolling river,
Oh Shenandoah I long to see you,
Away we're bound away
'Cross the wide Missouri.

The white man loved the Indian maiden,
Away you rolling river,
With notions his canoe was laden.
Away we're bound away
'Cross the wide Missouri.

Oh Shenandoah, I love your daughter,
Away you rolling river,
I'll take her 'cross the rolling water.
Away we're bound away
'Cross the wide Missouri.

Oh Shenandoah, I'm bound to leave you,
Away you rolling river,
Oh Shenandoah I'll not deceive you.
Away we're bound away
'Cross the wide Missouri.

Mountain man

Darling Nelly Gray

Thomas Jefferson's Louisiana Purchase stimulated many plantation owners to leave their worn-out land and migrate westward to Mississippi and Alabama. One of the results of this shift was the breakup of families among African-American slaves. These moves further aggravated the unhappy conditions of slavery. Uprisings, escapes and revolts increased. In his book *Fugitive Slaves In Canada*, published in 1856, Benjamin Drew quotes an ex-slave named Alexander Hamilton.

Hamilton said:

I knew one man to cut off the fingers of his left hand with an ax to prevent being sold south. I knew of another who on hearing he was sold, shot himself. I knew of a woman who had several children by her master, who on being sold, ran down to the river and drowned herself. Many separations I have seen, dragging husbands from wives, children from their mothers, and sending them where they could not expect to see each other again.

Along with Harriet Beecher Stowe's *Uncle Tom's Cabin*, B. R. Hanby's popular song "Darling Nelly Gray" proved effective in furthering the cause of abolition in the North.

Darling Nelly Gray

Words and Music: B. R. Hanby.

There's a low green valley on the old Kentucky shore, Where I've whiled many happy hours away, A-sitting and a-singing by the little cabin door Where dwelt my darling Nelly Gray. Oh my poor Nelly Gray, they have taken you away, And I'll never see my darling anymore, I'm sitting by the river and I'm weeping all the day, For you've gone from the old Kentucky shore.

There's a low green valley on the old Kentucky shore,
Where I've whiled many happy hours away,
A-sitting and a-singing by the little cabin door
Where dwelt my darling Nelly Gray.

CHORUS
Oh my poor Nelly Gray, they have taken you away,
And I'll never see my darling anymore,
I'm sitting by the river and I'm weeping all the day,
For you've gone from the old Kentucky shore.

When the moon had climbed the mountain, and the stars were
  shining too,
Then I'd take my darling Nelly Gray,
And we'd float down the river in my little red canoe,
While my banjo sweetly I would play.   CHORUS

One night I came to see her, but, "She's gone" the neighbors say,
"The white man bound her with his chain."
They have taken her to Georgia for to wear her life away
As she toils in the cotton and the cane.   CHORUS

My canoe is under water, and my banjo is unstrung,
I'm tired of living any more;
My eyes shall look downward and my song shall be unsung,
While I stay on the old Kentucky shore. CHORUS

My eyes are getting blinded and I cannot see the way,
Hark! There's somebody knocking at the door,
Oh, I hear the angels calling and I see my Nelly Gray,
Farewell to the old Kentucky shore.   CHORUS

LAST CHORUS
Oh my darling Nelly Gray up in heaven there, they say
That they'll never take you from me anymore,
I'm a coming, coming, coming, as the angels clear the way,
Farewell to the old Kentucky shore.

Slave auction

Steal Away

Secret meetings among slaves were often announced through the use of "signal songs" which used code words and symbolism. A widely used signal song from the 19th century was "Steal Away."

A Virginia slave named Nat Turner led a revolt in 1831 which, although ending in failure, sent shock waves through the slave-holding South. Some historians credit Nat Turner with authorship of "Steal Away."

Steal Away

Words and Music: Anonymous.

CHORUS
Steal away, steal away,
Steal away to Jesus.
Steal away, steal away,
I ain't got long to stay here.

My Lord calls me,
He calls me by the thunder,
The trumpet sounds it in my soul;
I ain't got long to stay here. CHORUS

Green trees are bending,
Poor sinners stand trembling;
The trumpet sounds it in my soul;
I ain't got long to stay here. CHORUS

My Lord calls me,
He calls me by the lightning;
The trumpet sounds it in my soul;
I ain't got long to stay here. CHORUS

Tombstones are bursting,
Poor sinners are trembling;
The trumpet sounds it in my soul;
I ain't got long to stay here. CHORUS

The capture of Nat Turner

Working on the plantation

The Abolitionist Hymn

The institution of slavery was always a divisive issue among white Americans. The strongest white opposition to slavery came from the Quakers. Benjamin Franklin was president of the Pennsylvania Society for Promoting the Abolition of Slavery, founded in 1775. By 1816, Quakers in North Carolina organized the General Association of the Manumission Society of North Carolina.

White abolitionists in the North organized anti-slavery singing societies. Ironically, many of these societies refused membership to African-American abolitionists. One of their best songs was "The Abolitionist Hymn." The melody is "Old Hundredth" (the hundredth psalm) from the *Genevan Psalter*, 1551.

The Abolitionist Hymn

Words and Music: Anonymous.

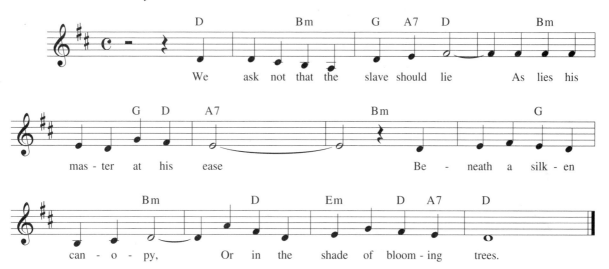

We ask not that the slave should lie
As lies his master at his ease
Beneath a silken canopy,
Or in the shade of blooming trees.

We ask not "eye for eye," that all
Who forge the chain and ply the whip
Should feel their torture, while the thrall
Should wield the scourge of mastership.

We mourn not that the man should toil,
'Tis nature's need, 'tis God's decree,
But let the hand that tills the soil
Be like the wind that fans it, free!

Follow the Drinking Gourd

The most effective organization involving black/white cooperation was the "underground railroad." Signal songs and code songs increased during this period. Words like Jesus, Canaan and Jordan meant "freedom," "the North" and "Canada." Songs like "Get On Board, Little Children," "Oh, Mary Don't You Weep Don't You Mourn" and "Follow the Drinking Gourd" were used to pass the word about a secret meeting or a successful escape. The "Drinking Gourd" was the Big Dipper constellation, with its two stars forming the end of the cup pointing to the North and freedom.

John and Alan Lomax, in their book *American Ballads and Folksongs*, relate the story of a one-legged sailor called Peg Leg Joe who taught escaping slaves this song. Joe left a trail marked with a left footprint and a round hole to follow as escapees made their way north to Ohio.

Follow the Drinking Gourd

Words and Music: Anonymous.

When the sun comes out and the first quail calls,
Follow the drinkin' gourd,
For the old man is a-waitin' for to carry you to freedom if you follow the drinkin' gourd.

CHORUS
Follow, follow, follow,
Follow the drinkin' gourd,
For the old man is a-waitin' for to carry you to freedom if you follow the drinkin' gourd.

The river bank makes a mighty good road,
The dead trees will show you the way,
Left foot, peg foot, travellin' on, follow the drinkin' gourd.   CHORUS

The river ends between two hills,
Follow the drinkin' gourd,
There's another river on the other side if you follow the drinkin' gourd.   CHORUS

Where the great big river meets the little river,
Follow the drinkin' gourd,
And the old man is a-waitin' for to carry you to freedom if you follow the drinkin' gourd.   CHORUS

Texas and the Mexican War

The Alamo

Cielito Lindo

The story of the Southwest, from Texas to California, is inseparable from the story of Mexico. Most Americans of Mexican descent can trace their ancestry back to Spain, and/or to one or more of Mexico's native peoples: Mayas, Aztecs, Yaquis, Zapotecs, Mixtecs, and many others.

Before the arrival of the Conquistadores, each Indian nation in Mexico had a unique musical tradition. After the Spanish conquest of Mexico, the music of Spain mixed with the music of the native Mexicans, and each region developed its own special sounds. The cultural backgrounds of Americans of Mexican descent are as varied as the two versions of the song "Cielito Lindo."

The first version is *norteño*, a musical style popular in northern Mexico and the southwestern United States. The second version is a *huapango*. A *huapango* is a popular dance in southern Mexico, and the songs that accompany the dance are also called *huapangos*.

The words to the *norteño* version mean:

From the dark mountain they appear, a pair of forbidding black eyes. Ay, ay, ay, ay! Sing and don't cry, because hearts sing quickly, my love. That beauty mark near your mouth, give it to no one, because it is mine. If the bird that abandons his first nest finds it taken by another, he deserves it. Cupid shot an arrow into the air, and I was the one injured. If your mother tells you to close the door, jingle the key and leave it open. When you fall in love, look first where you place your eyes, so you won't cry later.

The market place

Cielito Lindo (Norteño)

Words and Music: Anonymous.

De la sierra morena, Cielito Lindo, vienen bajando,
Un par de ojitos negros, Cielito Lindo, de contrabando.

CHORUS
¡Ay, ay, ay, ay!
Canta y no llores,
Porque cantando se alegran,
Cielito Lindo, los corazones.

Ese lunar que tienes, Cielito Lindo, junto a la boca,
No se lo des a nadie, Cielito Lindo, que a mi me toca.   CHORUS

Pájaro que abandona, Cielito Lindo, su primer nido,
Si lo encuentra ocupado, Cielito Lindo, muy merecido.   CHORUS

Una flecha en el aire, Cielito Lindo, lanzo Cupido,
Y como fue jugando, Cielito Lindo, yo fui el herido.   CHORUS

Si tú mama te dice, Cielito Lindo, cierra la puerta,
Hasle ruido a la llave, Cielito Lindo, y déjala abierto.   CHORUS

Siempre que te enamores, Cielito Lindo, mira primero
Donde pones los ojos, Cielito Lindo, no llores luego.

LAST CHORUS
¡Ay, ay, ay, ay!
Mira primero,
Donde pones los ojos,
Cielito Lindo, no llores luego.

The words to the *huapango* mean:

Every Sunday I come to visit you. When will it be Sunday again, my love, so I can return? Ah, how I wish all week long that it was Sunday. Tree of hope, don't weaken. Don't let your eyes weep as I depart, because if I see tears in your eyes, I will not leave. If you doubt my feelings, open my heart with a knife, my love. Ah, but open it with care that you do not hurt yourself, because you are within me. Some say they feel no pain at parting. Tell whoever told you that to bid farewell to the one he loves, and then see how he feels as his tears are falling. Ay, ay, ay!

Cielito Lindo (Huapango)

Words and Music: Anonymous.

De domingo a domingo te vengo a ver,
Cuando será domingo Cielito Lindo para volver.
¡Ay, ay, ay, ay, ay! Yo bien quisiera,
Que toda la semana, Cielito Lindo, domingo fuera.
¡Ay, ay, ay!

Árbol de la esperanza, mantente firme,
Que no lloren tús ojos, Cielito Lindo, al despedirme,
¡Ay, ay, ay, ay, ay! Porque si miro,
Lágrimas en tús ojos, Cielito Lindo, no me despido.
¡Ay, ay, ay!

Si alguna duda tienes de mi pasión,
Abre con un cuchillo, Cielito Lindo, mi corazón,
¡Ay, ay, ay, ay, ay! Pero con tiento,
Que tu no te làstimes, Cielito Lindo, que estas dentro.
¡Ay, ay, ay!

Dicen que no se siente la despedida,
Dile al quien te lo cuente, Cielito Lindo, que se despida,
¡Ay, ay, ay, ay, ay! Del ser que adora,
Y veras que lo siente, Cielito Lindo, y hasta que llora.
¡Ay, ay, ay!

El Capotin

During the Revolution of 1810 to 1821 Spain lost control of Mexico. Under Mexican rule the Southwest developed a culture famous for its hospitality, warmth, sociability and lively music.

Keith McNeil's father, Willard McNeil, learned "El Capotin" in 1898 when he was a small boy in Pozo, California. A capotin is a thatch of leaves worn over the shoulders to keep off the rain.

The words say:

With the *capotin*, it's going to rain tonight, and maybe again at dawn. I'm bound to love you, and I'm faithful. Ah, the troubles of a man who loves a woman. It's tough on a man when he falls in love. He drinks wine, gets drunk, goes to bed without any food. Don't kill me with a pistol or a knife, kill me with your eyes, and your red lips.

Mexican don

El Capotin

Words and Music: Anonymous.

Yo soy fir-me pa-ra a-mar-te, Y con-stan-te en el que-rer, Que tra-ba-jos, pa-sa un hom-bre, Cuan-do quie-re á un-a mu-jer. Con el ca-po-tin-tin-tin-tin, Que es-ta no-che va llo-ver, Con el ca-po-tin-tin-tin-tin, Que se-rá al a-man-e-cer. Con el ca-po-tin-tin-tin-tin, Que es-ta no-che va llo-ver, Con el ca-po-tin-tin-tin-tin, Que se-rá al a-ma-ne-cer.

Yo soy firme para amarte,
Y constante en el querer,
Que trabajos, pasa un hombre,
Cuando quiere á una mujer.

CHORUS
Con el capotin-tin-tin-tin,
Que esta noche va llover,
Con el capotin-tin-tin-tin,
Que será al amanecer.
Con el capotin-tin-tin-tin,
Que esta noche va llover,
Con el capotin-tin-tin-tin,
Que será al amanecer.

Que trabajos pasa un hombre
Cuando empieza á enamorar,
Toma vino, se emborracha,
Y se acuesta sin cenar. CHORUS

No me mates, no me mates,
Con pistola ni puñal,
Matame con tus ojitos,
Ó esos labios de coral. CHORUS

The Texas Rangers

The same year that Mexico won independence from Spain, a small group of Americans led by Stephen F. Austin moved into Texas. The newly created Mexican Republic welcomed the American settlers, but the Native Americans did not. As Austin's settlement grew, hostilities increased.

Settlers were protected from the Comanches by a small group of fighting men who called themselves Texas Rangers. At first the Comanches held the advantage. It took a full minute for a Ranger to reload his single shot muzzle-loading rifle. During that same minute, a fast-riding Comanche could shoot 20 arrows. The Comanches would surround the Rangers and draw their fire by shooting arrows. While the Rangers were reloading, the Comanches would ride in and finish them off with their fourteen-foot lances.

This Texas folk song dates back to the 1830s.

Texas Rangers

The Texas Rangers

Words and Music: Anonymous.

Come all you Tex - as Ran - gers wher - ev - er you may be, I hope you'll pay at - ten - tion and lis - ten un - to me, My name is noth - ing ex - tra the truth to you I'll tell, I am a rov - in' Ran - ger and I'm sure I wish you well.

Come all you Texas Rangers wherever you may be,
I hope you'll pay attention and listen unto me,
My name is nothing extra the truth to you I'll tell,
I am a rovin' Ranger and I'm sure I wish you well.

'Twas at the age of sixteen I joined this jolly band,
We marched from San Antonio unto the Rio Grande.
Our captain he informed us, perhaps he thought it right,
"Before we reach the station, boys, I'm sure we'll have to fight."

I saw the Indians comin' I heard them give a yell,
My feelings at that moment no human tongue can tell,
I saw their glittering lances, their arrows 'round me flew,
And all my strength it left me, and all my courage, too.

We fought a full nine hours before the strife was o'er,
The like of dead and wounded I never saw before,
And as the sun was risin' and the Indians they had fled,
We loaded up our rifles and counted up our dead.

Now all of us were wounded, our noble captain slain,
The sun was shinin' sadly across the bloody plain,
Sixteen brave Rangers as ever roamed the west
Were buried by their comrades with arrows in their breast.

I have seen the fruits of ramblin' I know its hardships well,
I have crossed the Rocky Mountains, rode down the streets of hell,
I have been in the Great Southwest where wild Apaches roam
And I'll tell you from experience you'd better stay at home.

In 1836, Samuel Colt developed a five-shot revolver called the Paterson. With the help of a Texas Ranger, Samuel Walker, Colt's handgun evolved into the Walker-Colt six-shooter. The Walker-Colt was a very large revolver, with a great deal more stopping power than the Paterson. The Texas Rangers adopted the new weapon, and the balance of power shifted from the Comanches to the Rangers.

The Texas War Cry

As more Americans moved into Texas in the 1830s, many of them did not take their Mexican citizenship seriously, and openly pressed for independence from Mexico. Tensions increased and escalated into armed conflict when President General Antonio López de Santa Anna marched into Texas.[4]

On March 2, 1836, at Washington on the Brazos, the Anglo-Texans signed their declaration of independence, creating the Republic of Texas. They sang "The Texas War Cry" to the tune of "The Star Spangled Banner."[5]

The Texas War Cry

Words: Anonymous. Music: John Stafford Smith.

[4] During the siege at the Alamo, Davy Crockett played his fiddle in duet with John McGregor who played his bagpipes, to keep up the spirits of the defenders.

[5] In his book *Sound off! Soldier Songs* Edward Arthur Dolph published "The Texas War Cry," and a number of other songs from the Mexican War, which he found in *The Rough and Ready Songster*, a small volume from the period.

Oh Texans rouse hill and dale with your cry,
No longer delay, for the bold foe advances,
The banners of Mexico tauntingly fly,
And the valleys are lit with the gleam of their lances.
With justice our shield, rush forth to the field,
And ne'er quit your post till our foes fly or yield,
For the bright star of Texas shall never grow dim,
While her soil boasts a son to raise rifle or limb.

Rush forth to the lines these hirelings to meet,
Our lives and our homes we will yield unto no man,
But death on our free soil we'll willingly meet,
Ere our free temple's soiled by the feet of the foeman,
Grasp rifle and blade, with hearts undismayed,
And swear by the temple brave Houston has made,
That the bright star of Texas shall never be dim,
While her soil boasts a son to raise rifle or limb.

The soldiers also sang "We're the Boys for Mexico," to the tune "Yankee Doodle:"

The Mexicans are doomed to fall,
God has in wrath forsook 'em,
And all their goods and chattels call
On us to go and hook 'em.
We're the boys for Mexico,
Sing Yankee Doodle Dandy,
Gold and silver images,
Plentiful and handy.

Sam Houston at the battle of San Jacinto

Will You Come to the Bower?

According to legend, Sam Houston's army marched into the battle of San Jacinto to the tune of "Will You Come to the Bower?" because Davy Crockett had sung the same song during the siege at the Alamo. The Battle of San Jacinto took place on April 21, 1836, just six weeks after the Texans' defeat at the Alamo. When Mexican General Santa Anna positioned his forces on a small semi-island in the San Jacinto River, Sam Houston decided to attack. His soldiers killed 600 of the 1,250 Mexican forces. Houston's army suffered only nine deaths.

Will You Come to the Bower?

Words and Music: Anonymous.

Will you come to the bower I have shaded for you?
Your bed shall be of roses bespangled with dew.
Will you, will you, will you, will you come to the bower?
Will you, will you, will you, will you come to the bower?

There under the bower on soft roses you lie
With a blush on your cheek, but a smile in your eye.
Will you, will you, will you, will you smile, my beloved?
Will you, will you, will you, will you smile, my beloved?

But the roses we press shall not rival your lips,
Nor the dew be so sweet as the kisses we'll sip.
Will you, will you, will you, will you kiss me my beloved?
Will you, will you, will you, will you kiss me my beloved?

And oh, for the joys that are sweeter than dew
From languishing roses or kisses from you.
Will you, will you, will you, will you, won't you, my love?
Will you, will you, will you, will you, won't you, my love?

Zachary Taylor

The new Texas Republic existed for nearly ten years as an independent nation before being admitted into the Union as a state on December 29, 1845. However, Mexico and the United States disagreed on the location of the western border of Texas. When Zachary Taylor's army advanced to the Rio Grande, Mexican forces crossed the river and attacked. After the battle, the United States declared war on Mexico. The hero of the Mexican War on the American side was Brigadier General and future president Zachary Taylor. His nickname was "Old Rough and Ready," and many of the songs sung by the American soldiers during the war extolled Taylor's virtues.

The words to "Zachary Taylor" were printed in *The Rough and Ready Songster*.

Zachary Taylor

Zachary Taylor

Words and Music: Anonymous.

Zach-ar-y Tay-lor was a brave old fel-ler, Brig-a-dier Gen'-ral,

A num-ber one, He fought twen-ty thou-sand Mex-i-can-os,

Four thou-sand he killed, the rest they cut and run.

Mat-a-mor-os he dis-turbed with A-mer-i-can thun-der,

Knocked their hous-es and their sol-diers down, And when the in-hab-it-ants had knocked

un-der, Struck up Yan-kee Doo-dle and he marched in-to town.

Zachary Taylor was a brave old feller,
Brigadier Gen'ral, A, number one,
He fought twenty thousand Mexicanos,
Four thousand he killed, the rest they cut and run.
Matamoros he disturbed with American thunder,
Knocked their houses and their soldiers down,
And when the inhabitants had knocked under,
Struck up Yankee Doodle and he marched into town.

Arista was the first that he gave fits to,
Just this side of the Rio Grand-ee,
Resaca de Palma and Palo Alto
Proved to the Mexicanos they couldn't come to tea.
Camargo was the place where he next went to,
The individuals there received him well,
They wheeled up their flour and their vegetables,
And other fixins they had a mind to sell.

To Monterrey then he turned his attention,
Ousted 'leven thousand, every mother's son,
When the Yankee nation come for to hear it,
They very much applauded what he had done.
To Saltillo town he introduced himself,
Marched right in and he made himself at home,
Then he got word that the valiant Santa Anna
To that place he had a mind to come.

Twelve miles old Rough and Ready traveled out to meet him,
At Buena Vista Pass they had a bloody fight,
Santa Anna and his army had a touch of Yankee mettle
That showed them "the elephant"[6] just about right.
In the thickest of the fight old Zachary appeared,
The shot flew about him as hot as any hail,
But the only injury that he received
Was a compound fracture of his brown coattail.

Long live old Zachary and his brave army!
Three times three, now give them a shout!
To punish all the foes wherever they are sassy,
Yankee volunteers are always about!
Yes, Yankee volunteers are always about!

[6] "The elephant" is a reference to the popular 19th century phrase "Seeing the Elephant." George Wilkins Kendall's *Santa Fe Expedition*, 1844, says: "When a man is disappointed in anything he undertakes, when he has seen enough, when he gets sick and tired of any job he may have set himself about, he has seen the elephant."

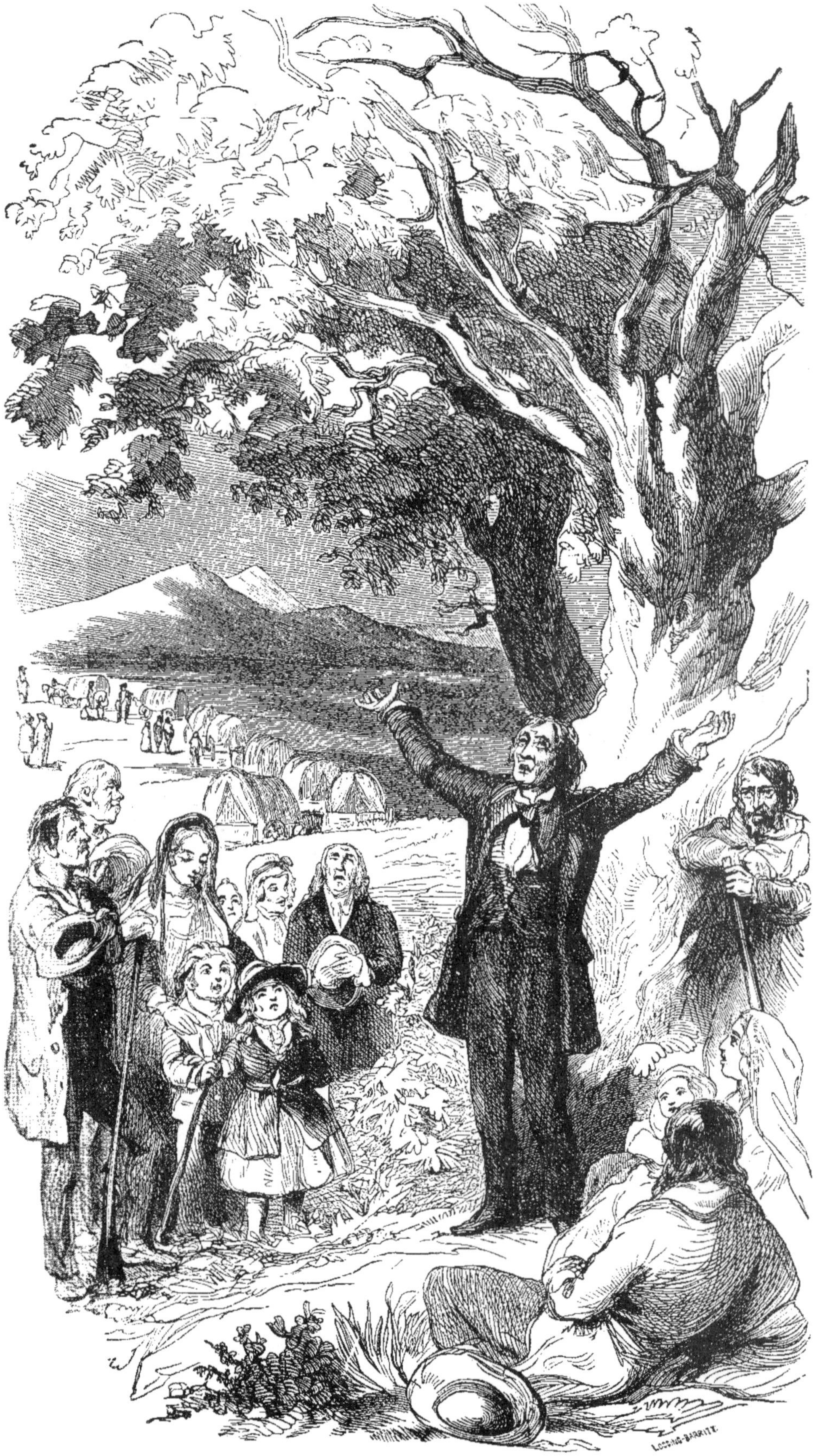

Mormons move west

The Mormon Battalion Song

One of the notable events of the Mexican War was the march of the Mormon Battalion. In 1846, the year the Mexican War began, persecution from neighboring communities had forced the Mormons to abandon their homes in Nauvoo, Illinois. When President Polk asked for volunteers to fight in the Mexican War, five hundred of the Mormon men traveling west with Brigham Young formed the now famous Mormon Battalion. They left their families on the trail and marched across the American continent from Iowa to the Pacific Ocean, more than two thousand miles.

"The Mormon Battalion Song" is an abridged version of a poem written by Eliza Snow, who later married Brigham Young. She called her poem *The Mormon Battalion, and the First Wagon Road Over the Great American Desert*. The poem was first published in 1881.

The Mormon Battalion Song

Words: Eliza R. Snow. Music: Anonymous.

When Mormon trains were journeying through to winter quarters from Nauvoo,
Five hundred men were called to go to settle claims with Mexico.
To fight for that same government from which as fugitives we went.
What were our families to do, our children, wives and mothers too?
When fathers, husbands, sons were gone, the dames drove teams and camp moved on.

And on the brave battalion went with Colonel Allen who was sent,
And well old Colonel Allen knew his Mormon boys were brave and true,
And he was proud of his command as he led forth his Mormon band.
Took sick and he died and we were left of a valiant leader soon bereaved.
And his successors proved to be the embodiment of cruelty.

Lieutenant Smith, the tyrant, led the battalion on in Allen's stead
To Santa Fe where Colonel Cook the charge of our battalion took.
'Twas well the vision of the way was closed to us at Santa Fe.
Because no infantry till then had ever suffered like us men.
Our rations were gone long weeks before we neared that great Pacific shore.

Our teams fell dead upon the road, our soldiers had to pull the load.
We found road-making worse by far than all the horrors of the war.
The enemy was panic struck, they dared not compete with Mormon pluck,
And off in all directions they fled, no charge was fired, no blood was shed.
And Colonel Cook himself well knew we Mormon men were brave and true.

Our God who rules in worlds by light controls by wisdom and by might.
The wise can see and understand while fools ignore his guiding hand.
'Twas thus predicted by the tongue of our great leader, Brigham Young,
"If to your God and country true you'll have no fighting there to do."
And thus with God Almighty's aid the conquest and the roads were made.

Buck Him and Gag Him

In contrast to the Mormon Battalion, the bulk of the volunteer army that fought in the Mexican War was largely undisciplined. Punishment for offences was severe, and hangings were frequent. Another common punishment was "bucking and gagging." The prisoner was spread-eagled face up on the ground, his arms and legs tied to stakes, and a gag stuffed into his mouth. As this song suggests, the soldiers deeply resented this punishment.

The tune is the traditional English folk melody "Down, Derry, Down."

The fight in the streets of Monterrey

Buck Him and Gag Him

Words and Music: Anonymous.

Come all Yan-kee sol-diers give ear to my song, It is a short dit-ty, it-'ll not keep you long, It's of no use to fret on ac-count of our luck, We can laugh, drink and sing yet, in spite of the buck! Drink her down, down, down drink her down!

Come all Yankee soldiers give ear to my song,
It is a short ditty, it'll not keep you long,
It's of no use to fret on account of our luck,
We can laugh, drink and sing yet, in spite of the buck!
Drink her down, down, down drink her down!

"Sergeant buck him and gag him!" our officers cry,
For each trifling offence which they happen to spy.
Till with bucking and gagging of Dick, Tom, Pat and Bill,
Faith, the Mexican's ranks they have helped to fill,
Drink her down, down, down drink her down!

The treatment they give us, as all of us know,
Is bucking and gagging for whipping the foe.
They buck us and gag us for malice or spite,
But they're glad to release us when it's time to fight,
Drink her down, down, down drink her down!

A poor soldier tied up in the hot sun or rain,
With a gag in his mouth till he's tortured with pain,
Why, I'm blest if the eagle we wear on our flag
In its claws couldn't carry a buck and a gag,
Drink her down, down, down drink her down!

The Leg I Left Behind Me

In 1838, General Antonio López de Santa Anna lost his leg in what came to be known as the "French Pastry War." Mexican soldiers had broken into a French pastry shop in Veracruz, Mexico, helping themselves to the pastries. The French baker demanded compensation. When the Mexican government ignored the demand, French warships entered Veracruz harbor and fired on the city. The last volley from the French shot off Santa Anna's leg.

Nine years later, at the Battle of Cerro Gordo during the Mexican War, three American soldiers from Pekin, Illinois, surprised Santa Anna. He retreated, leaving his carriage behind, which contained his cork leg and $18,000 in gold. The three American soldiers returned the money, but took the cork leg back to Illinois. The general's leg now resides in the Illinois National Guard Museum, in Springfield.

American soldiers couldn't resist writing and singing "The Leg I Left Behind Me," to the tune of the Irish song "The Girl I Left Behind Me."

Antonio López de Santa Anna

The Leg I Left Behind Me

Words and Music: Anonymous.

At Cerro Gordo my hopes were dashed, my scattered troops remind me.
'Twas there I got so soundly thrashed that I left my leg behind me.
I dare not go to view the place, lest Yankee foes should find me,
And mocking shake before my face the leg I left behind me!

Las Mañanitas

At the end of the Mexican War in 1848, Mexico ceded 525,000 square miles of territory to the United States. Many thousands of Mexican citizens remained to become American citizens. Mexico's influence on the Western states was, and remains, profound. The Spanish language, Mexican cattle ranching tools and techniques, place names, foods, architecture, land laws, clothing styles, music and dance, continue to be integral parts of the western American lifestyle.

The traditional morning birthday song "Las Mañanitas," originally from Jalisco, Mexico, is one of the many songs that remain popular in the southwestern United States.

The words say:

All the flowers were born on the day you were born, and all the nightingales sang. The dawn is coming, awake my beloved. I'd like to be a sunbeam entering your window to say good morning before you get up. I'd give a peso for the moon, half a peso for the sun, but I'd give my life and my heart to you. I'd like to take two stars from the skies, one to greet you, the other to say farewell.

Las Mañanitas

Words and Music: Anonymous.

El día en que tu nacis-te Nacie-ron to-das las flo-res. El día en que tu na-cis-tes Can-ta-ron los rui-se-ñor-es. Ya vie-ne ama-ne-cien-do, Ya la luz del día nos vió Ya des-pier-ta, ami-go mí-a, Mi-ra que ya ama-ne-ce.

El día en que tu naciste
Nacieron todas las flores.
El día en que tu nacistes
Cantaron los ruiseñores.
Ya viene amaneciendo,
Ya la luz del día nos vió
Ya despierta, amigo mía,
Mira que ya amanece.

Quisiera ser solecito
Para entrar por tu ventana
Y darte los buenos días
Acostadito en tu cama.
Por la luna doy un peso,
Por el sol doy un tostón,
Por mi amiga María
La vida y el corazón.

De las estrellas del cielo
Quisiera bajarte dos,
Una para saludarte
Y otra pa decirte adiós.

At the war's end, what many considered to be America's "Manifest Destiny," a country extending from the Atlantic Ocean to the Pacific Ocean, was now realized. Acquisition of this new territory, however, intensified the quarrels in the United States between the North and the South over free state versus slave state. In addition, the Mexican War itself proved to be a training ground for Ulysses S. Grant, Robert E. Lee, William Tecumseh Sherman, Thomas Jonathan "Stonewall" Jackson, George B. McClellan and Jefferson Davis, all of whom would become major figures in America's Civil War.

Minstrel Shows and the California Gold Rush

Old Dan Tucker

Though the 19th century minstrel show with its exaggerated characters in black-face is extremely offensive to our 21st century sensibilities, and promoted racial and cultural stereotypes that survived throughout the 20th century, it was perhaps the most popular form of entertainment among 19th century European-Americans. The minstrel shows spawned a body of American folksongs and melodies, composed by such well-known songwriters as Stephen Foster and Dan Decatur Emmett, that are still popular today.

As Americans migrated westward, the minstrel show followed. Dan Decatur Emmett composed "Dixie's Land," which became the anthem of the South, and "Old Dan Tucker," which became the most popular of all the minstrel songs.

Old Dan Tucker

Words and Music: Dan Decatur Emmett.

I come to town the other night, I heard the noise and I saw the fight,
The watchman was a-runnin' 'round sayin', "Old Dan Tucker's come to town."

CHORUS
Get out of the way, old Dan Tucker, get out of the way, old Dan Tucker,
Get out of the way, old Dan Tucker, you're too late to get your supper.

Old Dan Tucker was a fine old man, he washed his face with a fryin' pan,
Combed his hair with a wagon wheel, died with a tooth-ache in his heel. CHORUS

Now old Dan Tucker's comin' to town, he's swingin' the ladies 'round and 'round,
First to the right, then to the left, then to the gal that he loves best, so CHORUS

Old Dan Tucker he got drunk, fell in the fireplace, kicked up a chunk,
A red hot coal got in his shoe and whoo! how the ashes flew. CHORUS

Camptown Races

A minstrel show usually began with a grand march led by black-faced end men Tambo and Bones. The black-faced singers and dancers would file in and form a semi-circle. Then the interlocutor (master of ceremonies) would enter, take his position at center stage, say, "Gentlemen be seated," and make a speech praising the fame and virtue of the company. The show would begin with jokes and banter between the end men and the interlocutor, then move on to singing, dancing and instrumental music featuring banjo, tambourine and bones. Popular minstrel songs like "Old Dan Tucker," "Dixie," "Oh, Susannah" and "Camptown Races" swept the country.

American composer Stephen Foster grew up with minstrel music. As a child he loved to play "theater," which to him meant black-faced comedy. When he was nine years old he was part of a thespian company, and made quite a hit singing minstrel songs "Zip Coon," "Long-tailed Blue," "Jim Crow" and "Coal Black Rose."

As an adult, Foster composed a number of popular minstrel songs. His "Camptown Races" was published in 1850 under the title "Gwine to Run All Night." The title page of the publication read: FOSTER'S PLANTATION MELODIES, AS SUNG BY THE CHRISTY MINSTRELS. NO.1. OH LEMUEL, NO.2. DOLLY DAY, NO. 3. GWINE TO RUN ALL NIGHT, NO. 4. ANGELINA BAKER.

Camptown Races

Words and Music: Stephen Foster.

The Camptown ladies sing this song, duda, duda,
The Camptown race track five miles long, oh, duda day.
I come down there with my hat caved in, duda, duda,
And I go back home with a pocketful of tin, oh, duda day.

CHORUS
Goin' to run all night, goin' to run all day,
I'll bet my money on the bobtail nag, somebody bet on the bay.

The long tailed filly and the big black hoss, duda, duda,
They fly the track and they both get across, oh, duda day.
The blind hoss stickin' in a big mud hole, duda, duda,
Can't touch bottom with a ten foot pole, oh, duda day. CHORUS

Ole mulley cow come on to the track, duda, duda,
The bobtail fling her over his back, oh, duda day.
Then fly along like a railroad car, duda, duda,
Runnin' a race with a shootin' star, oh, duda day. CHORUS

See them flyin on a ten mile heat, duda, duda,
'Round the race-track then repeat, oh duda day.
I won my money on the bobtail nag, duda, duda,
And I'll keep my money in an old towbag, oh, duda day. CHORUS

Hard Times Come Again No More

Stephen Foster became the best of the minstrel songwriters. In addition to "Camptown Races," his songs included "Ring the Banjo," "My Old Kentucky Home" and "Oh, Susannah." Many of his minstrel tunes quickly entered the mainstream of American folksong. Miners used them for their gold rush songs, soldiers used them for their songs in the Mexican War and Civil War, and politicians did the same for their political songs.

However, Foster did not confine his efforts to minstrel songs. His "Jeanie With the Light Brown Hair," "Beautiful Dreamer" and "Old Folks at Home" are still international favorites.

Foster's parents were Northerners, ardent Democrats, and disapproved of the abolitionists. However, when Foster was growing up in Pittsburgh, Pennsylvania, his parents did allow Olivia Pise, the family "bound girl," to take young Stephen to her African-American church on Sundays. Foster was captivated by the music, and used the melodies for some of his songs, including "Oh, Boys, Carry Me 'Long," and "Hard Times Come Again No More."[7]

[7] "Hard Times Come Again No More" was parodied many times. Mormons sang "Brigham's Hard Times Come Again No More," and during the Civil War soldiers in the Union army sang "Hard Crackers Come Again No More."

Hard Times Come Again No More

Words: Stephen Foster. Music: Anonymous.

Let us pause in life's pleasures and count its many tears,
While we all sup sorrow with the poor.
There's a song that will linger forever in our ears,
"Oh, hard times come again no more."

CHORUS:
It's the song, the sigh of the weary,
"Hard times, hard times, come again no more,
Many days you have lingered around my cabin door,
Oh, hard times come again no more."

While we seek mirth and beauty, and music light and gay,
There are frail forms fainting at the door.
Though their voices are silent, their pleading looks will say,
"Oh, hard times come again no more." CHORUS

There's a pale, drooping maiden who toils her life away,
With a worn heart whose better days are o'er.
Though her voice would be merry, 'tis sighing all the day,
"Oh, hard times come again no more." CHORUS

It's a dirge that is wafted across the lonely seas,
It's a wail that is heard upon the shore.
It's a sigh that is murmured around the lonely grave,
"Oh, hard times come again no more." CHORUS

Oh, California

Stephen Foster's most productive song-writing years began in the late1840s. Foster's songs moved west with the wagon trains, and around Cape Horn on the ships. When gold was discovered in California in 1848, his "Oh, Susannah" became the anthem of the gold rush. The first of many gold rush parodies of Foster's "Oh, Susannah," was "Oh, California." John Nichols wrote "Oh, California" on board the ship *Eliza* in 1848, headed for California's gold fields.[8]

Oh, California

Words: John Nichols. Music: Stephen Foster.

I sailed from Salem City with my wash-bowl on my knee, I'm goin' to California, the gold dust for to see. It rained all night the day I left, the weather it was dry, The sun so hot I froze to death, oh brothers don't you cry!

chorus Oh, California, that's the land for me! I'm goin' to San Francisco with my wash-bowl on my knee.

[8] California miners were not alone in their enthusiasm for "Oh, Susannah." The following song was published in *The Millenial Star* August 15, 1857. It was written and sung to the tune "Oh, Susannah" by Mormon missionaries as they pushed their handcarts from Salt Lake City, Utah, to Florence, Nebraska:

No purse, no script they bear with them, but cheerfully they start
And cross the plains a thousand miles and draw with them a cart.
Ye nations list! the men of God, from Zion now they come,
Clothed with the Priesthood and the Power, they gather Israel home.

I sailed from Salem City with my washbowl on my knee,
I'm goin' to California, the gold dust for to see.
It rained all night the day I left, the weather it was dry,
The sun so hot I froze to death, oh brothers don't you cry!

CHORUS
Oh, California, that's the land for me!
I'm goin' to San Francisco with my wash-bowl on my knee.

I jumped aboard the '*Liza* ship and traveled on the sea,
And every time I thought of home I wished it wasn't me!
The vessel reared like any horse that had of oats a wealth,
I found it wouldn't throw me, so I thought I'd throw myself! CHORUS

I thought of all the pleasant times we've had together here,
I thought I ought to cry a bit, but couldn't find a tear.
The pilot's bread was in my mouth, the gold dust in my eye,
And though I'm going far away, dear brothers don't you cry! CHORUS

I soon shall be in Frisco, and there I'll look around,
And when I find the gold lumps there I'll pick them off the ground.
I'll scrape the mountains clean, my boys, I'll drain the rivers dry,
A pocketful of rocks bring home, oh brothers don't you cry! CHORUS

Like Argos of the ancient times I'll leave this modern Greece,
I'm bound to California mines to find the golden fleece.
For who would work from morn till night, and live on hog and corn,
When one can pick up there at sight enough to buy a farm. CHORUS

There from the snowy mountainside comes down the golden sand,
And spreads a carpet far and wide o'er all the shining land.
The rivers run on golden beds o'er rocks of golden ore,
The valleys six feet deep are said to hold a plenty more. CHORUS

I'll take my wash-bowl in my hand and thither wind my way,
To wash the gold from out the sand in California.
And when I get my pocket full in that bright land of gold,
I'll have a rich and happy time, live merry till I'm old. CHORUS

Washing for gold in the Sierra Nevada foothills

Crossing the Plains

The discovery of gold touched off a wild race to California. Men left families, farms and businesses to search for the precious yellow metal. In two years, from January 1848 to January 1850, California's non-Indian population grew from 30,000 to 200,000. Emigrants gathered in April and May at Independence, Westport and St. Joseph, Missouri to join wagon trains. The covered wagons were mostly Conestoga wagons manufactured in the east, and were soon nicknamed "prairie schooners." A typical load for each adult included 200 pounds of flour, 30 pounds of pilot bread, 75 pounds of bacon, 25 pounds of sugar, plus rice, coffee, tea and beans. Teams were made up of 10 to 12 horses or mules, or 12 oxen. Here's an excerpt from the diary of a forty-niner:

May 3rd, 1849. Fifteen miles to Bull Creek. The guide pointed out the continuous rise and fall of the track across what are rightly called the billows, or little ridges of the prairie. "No, it's not high mountains ner great rivers ner hostile injuns," says Meek, "that'll give us most grief. It's the long grind o' doin' every day's work reglar an' not let-up fer nothin'. Figger it out fur yourself; two thousand one hundred miles - four months to do it in between April rains and September snows - 123 days. How much a day and every cussed day?" I saw the point. Seventeen miles a day.

"Yaas" drawled the scout. "And every day rain, hail, cholera, breakdowns, lame mules, sick cows, washouts, prairie fires, flooded coulees, lost horses, dust storms and alkali water. Seventeen miles every day or you land in the snow and eat each other like the Donner party done in '46."

May 13, 1849. Long pull. Here we are beginning to meet people who are turning back, discouraged. They had seen enough of the elephant. Graves are more frequent these last days. We saw whitening on the plains, bones of animals which had died on the way. (From Archer Butler Hulbert's '49ers, 1931)

"Crossing the Plains" was written by John A. Stone, and published in his *Put's Original California Songster* in 1855. Five editions of the songbook were published by D. E. Appleton & Co. between 1855 and 1870, selling twenty-five thousand copies. Stone's nickname (and pen name) was "Old Put." He came to California in 1850, struck it rich in 1853, and retired to write songs and play his guitar. He organized a singing group called the "Sierra Nevada Rangers" and they toured the mining camps singing Put's songs. Their popularity led to the publication of a number of gold rush songbooks in the 1850s.

Crossing the plains

Crossing the Plains

Words: John A. Stone. Music: Anonymous.

Come all you Cal - i - for - ni - ans I pray ope wide your ears, If you are go - ing a - cross the Plains with snot - ty mules and steers, Re - mem - ber beans be - fore you start, like - wise dried beef and ham, Be - ware of ve - ni - son, dang the stuff, it's of - ten times a ram.

Come all you Californians I pray ope wide your ears,
If you are going across the Plains with snotty mules and steers,
Remember beans before you start, likewise dried beef and ham,
Beware of venison, dang the stuff, it's often times a ram.

You must buy two revolvers, a bowie knife and belt,
Says you, "Old feller, now stand off, or I will have your pelt."
The greenhorn looks around about, but not a soul can see,
Says he, "There's not a man in town, but what's afraid of me."

Don't shave your beard but cultivate your down and let it grow.
And when you do return it will be as soft and white as snow,
Your lovely Jane will be surprised, your ma'll begin to cook,
The greenhorn to his mother'll say, "How savage I must look!"

"How do you like it overland?" his mother she will say,
"All right, excepting cooking, then the devil is to pay,
For some won't cook, and others can't, and then it's curse and damn,
The coffee pot's begun to leak, so has the frying pan."

You calculate on sixty days to take you over the Plains,
But when you lack for bread and beef, for coffee and for brains,
Your sixty days are a hundred or more, your grub you've got to divide,
Your steers and mules are alkalied, so foot it you cannot ride.

You have to stand a watch at night to keep the Indians off,
About sundown some heads will ache, and some begin to cough,
To be deprived of health we know is always very hard,
But every night someone is sick to get rid of standing guard.

Your canteens they should be well filled, with poison alkali,
So when you get tired of traveling, you can cramp right up and die.
The best thing in the world to keep your bowels loose and free
Is fight and quarrel among yourselves, and seldom if ever agree.

There's not a log to make a seat, along the river Platte,
So when you eat you've got to stand, or set down square and flat.
It's fun to cook with buffalo wood, take some that's newly born,
If I knew then what I know now, I'd of gone around the Horn.

The desert's nearly death on corns, while walking in the sand,
And drive a jackass by the tail, it's damn this overland,
I'd rather ride a raft at sea, and then at once be lost,
Says Bill, "Let's leave this poor old mule, we can't get him across."

The ladies have the hardest time, when they emigrate by land,
And when they cook with buffalo wood, they often burn a hand,
And then they jaw their husbands round, get mad and spill the tea,
I wish to God they'd be taken down with a turn of di-a-ree.

When you arrive at Placerville, or Sacramento City,
You haven't a cent to buy a meal, no money, what a pity.
Your striped pants are all wore out which causes people to laugh,
To see you gapin' round the town like a great big brindle calf.

You're lazy, poor, and all broke down, such hardships you endure,
The post office at Sacramento all such men will cure,
You'll find a line from ma and pa, and one from lovely Sal,
If that don't physic you every mail, you never will get well.

The Days of Forty-Nine

Some of the first gold seekers to arrive in California were from Hawaii, Mexico, Chile and Peru. Ships had carried the news of the discovery of gold to those countries before word reached the eastern seaboard. By 1849 about one out of every four gold seekers was from a country other than the United States. Whatever the nationality, life in the mining camps was not easy. The work was hard, the food terrible, and sleeping accommodations uncomfortable. After a grueling day's work, the evening was usually taken up with heavy drinking and gambling. The favorite games were three card monte, euchre and poker. The combination of homesickness, mixed ethnic and racial groups, heavy drinking and gambling resulted in frequent fights and killings.

The Days of Forty-Nine

Words: Charles Rhoades. Music: Anonymous.

I'm old Tom Moore, a bummer sure, of the good old golden days,
They call me a bummer and a gin sot too, but what care I for praise,
I wander around from town to town just like a ramblin' sign,
And the people all say, "There goes Tom Moore, of the days of forty-nine."

CHORUS
In the days of old, in the days of gold, how oft-times I repine,
In the days of old when we dug up the gold, in the days of forty-nine.

My comrades they all knew me well, a jolly, saucy crew,
A few hard cases I will admit, though they were brave and true,
Whatever the pinch they never would flinch, they never would fret or whine,
Like good old bricks they stood the kicks in the days of forty-nine.

There was old lame Jess, a hard old cuss, he never did repent,
He was never known to miss a drink, or ever spend a cent.
But old lame Jess, like all the rest, to death he did resign,
And in his bloom went up the flume in the days of forty-nine. CHORUS

There was New York Jake, the butcher's boy, he was always gettin' tight,
And every time that he'd get full he was lookin' for a fight.
Then Jake rampaged against a knife in the hands of old Bob Sine,
And over Jake we held a wake in the days of forty-nine.

There was ragshag Bill from Buffalo, I never will forget.
He would roar all day and he'd roar all night, and I guess he's roarin' yet.
One night Bill fell in a prospect hole in a roarin' bad design,
And in that hole Bill roared out his soul in the days of forty-nine. CHORUS

There was Kentuck Bill, one of the boys who was always in the game,
No matter whether he lost or won, to him it was all the same,
He'd ante a slug, he'd pass the buck, he'd go for a hat full blind,
In the game of death, Bill lost his breath in the days of forty-nine.

There was Monte Pete, I'll ne'er forget the luck he always had,
He'd deal for you both night and day, or as long as you had a scad.
One night a pistol laid him out, 'twas his last lay out in fine,
It caught Pete sure, right bang at the door, in the days of forty-nine. CHORUS

There was another chap from New Orleans, Big Reuben was his name,
On the plaza there with a sardine box he opened a faro game.
He dealt so fair that a millionaire he became in course of time,
Till death stepped in and called the turn in the days of forty-nine.

Of all the comrades that I've had there's none that's left to boast,
And I'm left alone in my misery like some poor wanderin' ghost.
And as I roam from town to town, they call me the ramblin' sign,
There goes Tom Moore, a bummer sure, of the days of forty-nine. CHORUS

Using the same tune, J. Riley Mains wrote a popular follow-up song called "The Good Old Days of '50, '1, and '2:"

Tom Moore has sung of '49, and the pioneers who came
Across the plains and 'round the Horn in search of gold and fame,
But in his song he tells us not one word of those we knew,
Those pioneers of the good old days of '50, '1, and '2.

There's Kentuck Bill and Monte Pete, he holds them up to fame,
New York Jake and Ransack Jim and Old Lame Jess the same,
But men like these were not the boys so hardy, tough and true,
That flumed the streams and worked the mines in '50, '1, and '2.

There's Captain Love and gallant Burns, Dave Buell tall and brave,
Likewise Bob Fall and also Thorn, were the dread of Robber's Cave.
They would trace them over the mountain steep, ravines and cañons through,
Those men of pluck in the good old days of '50, '1, and '2.

Where are they now, that gallant band, those friends that once were mine?
Some sleep beneath the willow's shade, some 'neath the lofty pine,
While some have sand beneath the wave deep in the ocean's blue,
Those cherished friends of bygone years of '50, '1, and '2.

I once had wealth. It brought new friends. I thought them true, I'll own,
But when kind fortune ceased to smile, those summer friends had flown,
And now I wander on alone life's thorny pathways through,
But I'll ne'er forget those dear old friends of '50, '1, and '2.

'Tis true there's some old pioneers that unto wealth have grown,
But there are many that are poor, and I am one, I'll own,
But never shun a ragged coat if the heart beneath is true,
Of a pioneer of the good old days of '50, '1, and '2.

And now, kind friends, I've sung my song, I've had my little speak,
But when I think of those good old days, tears often wet my cheek.
We opened then the Golden Gate and its treasures unto you,
We boys who came in '49, and in '50, '1, and '2.

Cripple Creek (Square Dance)

Sometimes the miners would have a dance, and the dancing often lasted all night long. When there were no women present in the camp, the miners danced with each other. Every man who wore a white patch on his pants was considered a lady. The caller would improvise to suit the situation.

The traditional southern banjo tune "Cripple Creek" is still a favorite among square dancers.

Cripple Creek (Square Dance)

Music: Anonymous

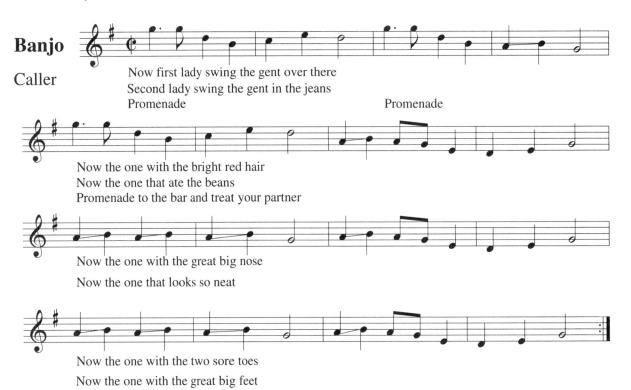

Banjo

Caller

Now first lady swing the gent over there
Second lady swing the gent in the jeans
Promenade   Promenade

Now the one with the bright red hair
Now the one that ate the beans
Promenade to the bar and treat your partner

Now the one with the great big nose

Now the one that looks so neat

Now the one with the two sore toes

Now the one with the great big feet

Caller: Now first lady swing the gent over there
          Now the one with the bright red hair
          Now the one with the great big nose
          And now the one with two sore toes

          Second lady swing the gent in the jeans
          Now the one that ate the beans
          Now the one that looks so neat
          Now the one with the great big feet.

          Promenade, promenade,
          Promenade to the bar and treat your partner!

California Ball

In camps where there was a female population, all of the women attended the dances - wives, mothers, children, grandchildren - regardless of age, ethnicity, occupation, reputation or marital status.

"Old Put" set these words to the tune of R. P. Buckley's then popular song "Wait For The Wagon."

California Ball

Words: John A. Stone. Music: R. P. Buckley.

The la-dies through the dig-gings wind, and o-ver moun-tains tall, With young ones tag-ging on be-hind flat-foot-ed for the ball. The man-a-ger be-gins to curse and swag-gers through the hall, For moth-ers they've gone out to nurse their ba-bies at the ball.

chorus
Wait for the mu-sic! Wait for the mu-sic! Wait for the mu-sic! And we'll all have a dance!

The ladies through the diggings wind, and over mountains tall,
With young ones tagging on behind flat-footed for the ball.
The manager begins to curse and swaggers through the hall,
For mothers they've gone out to nurse their babies at the ball.

CHORUS
Wait for the music! Wait for the music!
Wait for the music! And we'll all have a dance!

'Twould make our eastern people cave, to see the great and small,
The old, with one foot in the grave, all splurging at a ball.
A dozen babies on the bed and all begin to squall,
The mothers wish the brats were dead, for crying at the ball! CHORUS

Old women in their bloomer rigs are fond of "balance all."
And "weighty" when it comes to jigs, and so on, at the ball!
A yearling miss fills out the set, although not very tall,
"I'm anxious now," she says, "you bet, to proceed with the ball!" CHORUS

A married woman, gentle dove, with nary tooth at all,
Sits in the corner making love with a stranger at the ball!
The Spanish hags of ill repute for brandy loudly call,
And no one dares their right dispute to freedom at the ball! CHORUS

A drunken loafer at the dance informs them one and all,
With bowie knife stuck in his pants, "The best man at the ball!"
The gambler all the money wins, to bed the drunkest crawl,
And fighting then of course begins with rowdies at the ball! CHORUS

They rush it like a railroad car and often is the call
Of "Promenade up to the bar!" for whiskey at the ball!
"Old Alky" makes their bowels yearn, they stagger round and fall,
And ladies say when they return, "Oh, what a splendid ball!" CHORUS

Dance hall

Sweet Betsey From Pike

The women who traveled to California in the 1840s and '50s shared in the hardships of the journey. They were immortalized in the popular gold rush song "Sweet Betsey [sic] From Pike." The tune was originally "Villikens And His Dinah," an English music hall song composed by John Parry. The tune has dozens of parodies in England, Ireland and the United States.

"Sweet Betsey From Pike" was published in *Put's Golden Songster*.

Sweet Betsey From Pike

Words: John A. Stone. Music: John Parry.

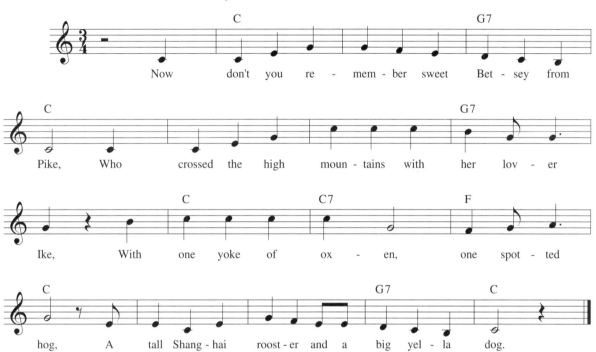

Now don't you re - mem - ber sweet Bet - sey from Pike, Who crossed the high moun - tains with her lov - er Ike, With one yoke of ox - en, one spot - ted hog, A tall Shang - hai roost - er and a big yel - la dog.

Now don't you remember sweet Betsey from Pike,
Who crossed the high mountains with her lover Ike,
With one yoke of oxen, one spotted hog,
A tall Shanghai rooster and a big yella dog.

One evenin' quite early they camped on the Platte,
'Twas nearby the road on a green shady flat,
Sweet Betsey grew weary, lay down to repose,
While Isaac stood gazin' at his Pike County rose.

They soon reached the desert where Betsey gave out;
And down in the sand she lay rollin' about,
Then Ike with great wonder looked on in surprise, sayin',
"Betsey, get up, you'll get sand in your eyes!"

They stopped at Salt Lake to inquire the way,
And Brigham he swore that sweet Betsey should stay,
Sweet Betsey got scairt and she run like a deer,
While Brigham stood pawin' the ground like a steer.

The Injuns come down in a wild yellin' horde,
And Betsey was scairt they would scalp her adored,
So behind the front wagon wheel Betsey did crawl,
And there she fought Injuns with musket and ball.

The horses ran off and the cattle all died,
And the last piece of bacon that mornin' was fried,
Poor Ike got discouraged, Betsey got mad,
The dog wagged his tail and looked wonderfully sad.

They climbed to the top of a very high hill,
And they stood lookin' down upon old Placerville,
Ike shouted and said as he cast his eyes down,
"Sweet Betsey, my darlin', we've got to Hangtown."

Long Ike and sweet Betsey attended a dance.
Ike wore a pair of his Pike County pants,
Sweet Betsey was dressed up in ribbons and rings,
Quoth Ike, "You're an angel, but where are your wings?"

A miner said, "Betsey, will you dance with me?"
"I will you old hoss, if you don't make too free,
But don't dance me hard, do you want to know why?
Doggone you I'm chuck full of old alkali."

The disparaging references to Brigham Young and Indians in the song reflect the prejudices common in California during the gold rush era. Mexicans, Chinese, Central Americans, South Sea Islanders and African-Americans were also targets of prejudice.

California As It Is

The gold rush proved to be a major disappointment to thousands of miners. While some of them struck it rich, most of them did not. This song was written by Thaddeus Meighan in 1849.

California As It Is

Words and Music: Thaddeus Meighan.

Oh I've been to Cal - i - for - nia and I have-n't got a dime, I've lost my health, my strength, my hope, and I have lost my time, I've on - ly got a spade and pick, and if I felt quite brave, I'd use the two of them there things to scoop me out a grave. This dig - gin' hard for gold may be pol - i - tic and bold, But you could not make me think so, but you may if you are told. Oh I've been to Cal - i - for - nia, and I'm mi - nus all the gold, For in - stead of rich - es plen - ty I have on - ly got a cold, And I think in go - ing min - ing I was reg - u - lar - ly sold.

Oh I've been to California and I haven't got a dime,
I've lost my health, my strength, my hope, and I have lost my time,
I've only got a spade and pick, and if I felt quite brave,
I'd use the two of them there things to scoop me out a grave.
This diggin' hard for gold may be politic and bold,
But you could not make me think so, but you may if you are told.
Oh I've been to California, and I'm minus all the gold,
For instead of riches plenty I have only got a cold,
And I think in going mining I was regularly sold.

I left this precious city with two suits of gallus rig,
My boots though India-rubber, were sufficiently big
For to keep the water out, as well as alligators,
And I tell you now my other traps were very small potatoes.
I had a great machine, the greatest ever seen
To wash the sands of value and to get the gold out clean,
And I had a fancy knapsack filled with sausages and ham,
And of California diggers, I went out "the great I am,"
But I found the expedition was a most confounded flam.

Now only listen to me and I'll tell you in a trice
That poking in the dirt for gold ain't more than very nice,
You're starved, stewed and frozen, and the strongest man he says he's
Bound to have your money, or he'll wallop you like blazes.
I was shot, and stabbed, and kicked, and remarkably well licked,
And compelled to eat poll parrots which were roasted but not picked.
And I slept beneath a tent which hadn't got a top,
With a ragged blanket 'round me and the ground all of a sop,
And for all this horrid suffering I haven't got a cop!

So here I am without a home, without a cent to spend,
No toggery, no vittles, and not a single friend,
With lizards, parrots, spiders, snakes and other things unclean
All crowded in my stomach, and I'm very weak and lean.
But I ain't the only one that's got tired of this here fun,
For about a dozen thousand chaps are ready now to run
As hard as they can possibly from there to kingdom come,
For there they ain't nobody, sir, but here they might be some,
And enjoy their cakes and coffee and now and then some rum.

If you've enough to eat and drink and buy your Sunday clothes,
Don't listen to the gammon that from California blows,
But stay at home and thank your stars for every hard-earned cent,
And if the greenhorns go to dig, why cooly let 'em went.
If you go, why you will see, the elephant, yes siree,
And some little grains of gold that are no bigger than a flea,
I've just come from California, and if any here there be
Who has got that yellow fever, they need only look at me,
And I think New York will suit 'em, yes, exactly to a T.

Outfitting in St. Louis, Missouri for the California gold fields

Immigrants from China, Ireland and Germany

The Heathen Chinee

Bret Harte settled in San Francisco in 1860, working as a journalist and printer. When he became editor of the *Overland Monthly*, he began publishing his "local color" stories. In September, 1870, he published his poem *Plain Language from Truthful James* about a Chinese immigrant named Ah Sin who outsmarts (and out-cheats) Bill Nye, the cardsharp, in a game of euchre. This poem, along with his *Luck of Roaring Camp*, *Outcast of Poker Flat*, *Tennessee's Partners*, *Miggles*, and *Brown of Calaveras*, catapulted Harte into national prominence. *Plain Language from Truthful James* was pirated by a number of publishers in the U.S. under the title *The Heathen Chinee*. Someone added a tune and "The Heathen Chinee" became a song.

Euchre is a card game similar to rummy or pinochle. The two highest cards are the jack of the trump suit and the jack of the same color. These are the "right bower" and the "left bower" respectively. Euchre was a favorite game at the California mining camps.

Chinese immigrants at San Francisco's custom house

The Heathen Chinee

Words: Bret Harte. Music: Anonymous.

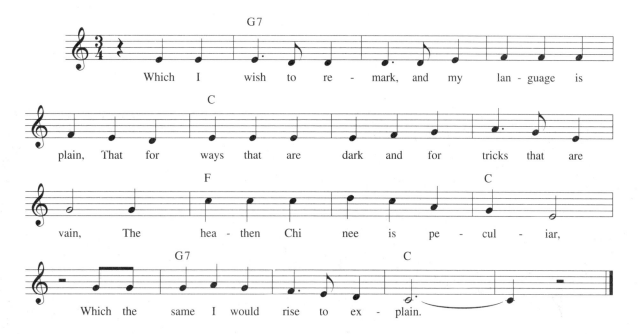

Which I wish to re - mark, and my lan - guage is plain, That for ways that are dark and for tricks that are vain, The hea - then Chi nee is pe - cul - iar, Which the same I would rise to ex - plain.

Which I wish to remark, and my language is plain,
That for ways that are dark and for tricks that are vain,
The heathen Chinee is peculiar,
Which the same I would rise to explain.

Ah Sin was his name, and I shall not deny
In regards to the same what that name might imply,
But his smile it was pensive and childlike,
As I frequent remarked to Bill Nye.

It was August the third and quite soft was the skies,
Which it might be inferred that Ah Sin was likewise,
But he played it that day upon William
And me, in the way I despise.

Which we had a small game, Ah Sin took a hand,
It was euchre, the same he did not understand,
But he smiled as he sat by the table,
With a smile that was childlike and bland.

Yet the cards they were stocked in a way which I grieve,
And my feelings were shocked at the state of Nye's sleeve
Which was stocked full of aces and bowers,
And the same with intent to deceive.

But the cards that were played by that heathen Chinee,
And the points that he made were quite frightful to see,
Till at last he lay down a right bower,
Which the same Nye had dealt unto me.

I looked up at Nye, and he gazed upon me,
And he rose with a sigh and he said, "Can this be?
We are ruined by Chinese cheap labor!"
And he went for that heathen Chinee.

In the scene that ensued I did not take a hand,
And the floor it was strewn like the leaves on the strand,
With the cards that Ah Sin had been hiding,
In a game he did not understand.

In his sleeves, which were long, we found twenty-four jacks,
Which is going it strong though I state but the facts,
And we found on his nails, which were tapered,
What is common to tapers, that's wax.

Which is why I remark, and my language is plain,
That for ways that are dark and for tricks that are vain,
The heathen Chinee is peculiar,
Which the same I am free to maintain.

John Chinaman

The gold rush attracted many immigrants from China. California's Chinese population increased from less than a thousand at the beginning of 1850 to 12,000 a year later, and to 50,000 by 1856. California governor John Mc Dougal, in his 1852 address to the legislature, encouraged Chinese immigration and settlement, referring to the Chinese as "one of the most worthy classes of our newly adopted citizens." The white miners, however, wanted California's gold for themselves, and the state's attitude toward the new Chinese immigrants quickly changed from welcome to hostility.

The state legislature established a foreign miners' tax of twenty dollars per month. Tuolumne County passed a law forbidding "Asiatics" and South Sea Islanders from mining for themselves or others. Mining communities posted notices ordering Chinese out of the districts. The Agua Fría District posted a notice in 1856 which read: "Notice is hereby given to all Chinese on the Agua Fría and its tributaries to leave within ten days from this date, and any failing to comply will be subjected to thirty-nine lashes and moved by force of arms."

Songs of the gold rush often reflected this anti-Chinese attitude. "John Chinaman" was published in the *California Songster*, 1856.

John Chinaman

Words and Music: Anonymous.

John Chinaman, John Chinaman but five short years ago,
I welcomed you from Canton, but I wish I hadn't though,
I imagined that the truth John you'd speak when under oath,
But I find you'll lie and steal too, yes, John you're up to both.

For then I thought you honest, John, not dreaming but you'd make
A citizen as useful, John, as any in the State.
I thought you'd cut your queue off, John, and don a Yankee coat,
And a collar high you'd raise, John, around your dusky throat.

I thought of rats and puppies, John, you'd eaten your last fill,
But on such slimy pot-pies I'm told you dinner still,
Yes, John I've been deceived in you, and in all your thieving clan,
For our gold is all you're after, John, to get it as you can.

John Chinaman's Appeal

In 1864, Mark Twain wrote a satirical article titled *The Disgraceful Persecution of a Boy* for the *Morning Call*, a San Francisco newspaper. The editor refused to print it. He told Twain that the paper was "the washerwoman's paper," supported by the poor, that the poor were Irish, and that the Irish hated the Chinese. He said without his Irish subscribers the newspaper would not last a month.

Twain's article was eventually published by Sheldon & Company in their New York magazine *The Galaxy*, in May, 1870.

In San Francisco the other day, "A well-dressed boy on his way to Sunday school was arrested and thrown into the city prison for stoning Chinamen..."

Before we side against him, let us give him a chance. Let us hear the testimony for the defense. He was a well-dressed boy, and a Sunday school scholar, and therefore the chances are that his parents were intelligent, well-to-do people with just enough natural villainy in their composition to make them yearn after the daily papers, and enjoy them. And so this boy had opportunities to learn all through the week how to do right, as well as on Sunday. It was in this way that he found out that the great commonwealth of California imposes an unlawful mining tax upon John, the foreigner, and allows Patrick, the foreigner, to dig gold for nothing. It was in this way that he found out that a respectable number of the tax-gatherers, it would be unkind to say all of them, collect the tax twice instead of once. And that, inasmuch as they do it solely to discourage Chinese immigration into the mines, it is a thing that is much applauded.

It was in this way that he found out that when a white man robs a sluice box they make him leave the camp, and when a Chinaman does that thing, they hang him...

It was in this way that the boy found out that a Chinaman had no rights that any man was bound to respect. That he had no sorrows that any man was bound to pity. That neither his life nor his liberty was worth the purchase of a penny when a white man needed a scapegoat. That nobody loved Chinamen, nobody befriended them, nobody spared them suffering when it was convenient to inflict it. Everybody, individuals, communities, the majesty of the state itself joined in hating, abusing and persecuting these humble strangers.

And therefore, what could have been more natural than for this sunny-hearted boy, tripping along to Sunday school, with his mind teeming with freshly learned incentives to high and virtuous action, to say to himself, "Ah, there goes a Chinaman. God will not love me if I do not stone him..."

"John Chinaman's Appeal," sung to the tune "Yankee Doodle," was a remarkably sympathetic song for the period. Nearly every other gold rush song that mentioned the Chinese reflected a negative attitude. The song also accurately incorporated a number of historical events experienced by Chinese miners.

Mart Taylor, saloonkeeper, singer and songwriter, wrote a number of gold rush songs, including "John Chinaman's Appeal," and published them in his book *The Gold Diggers' Songbook* in 1856. Taylor was also a minstrel show performer. His troupe was called Taylor's Original Minstrel Company.

The "long tom" in the song is a sluice box, measuring in length between 18 and 50 feet. It is used to separate the gold from sand and gravel. The "rocker" is a box on rockers. The rocking motion of the box agitates the sluice, separating the gold. The "cue" [*sic*] is the pigtail worn by the Chinese miners.

Mark Twain

John Chinaman's Appeal

Words: Mart Taylor. Music: Anonymous.

A - mer - i - can, now mind my song, if you would but hear

me sing, And I will tell you of the wrong that hap - pened un - to

Gee Sing. In fif - ty - two I left my home, I bid fare - well to

Hong Kong, And start-ed with Cup Gee to roam to the land where they use the "long tom."

American, now mind my song, if you would but hear me sing,
And I will tell you of the wrong that happened unto Gee Sing.
In fifty-two I left my home, I bid farewell to Hong Kong,
And started with Cup Gee to roam to the land where they use the "long tom."

In forty days I reached the bay, and nearly starved was I, sir,
I cooked and ate a dog one day, I did not know the laws, sir.
But soon I found my dainty meal was 'gainst the city order,
The penalty I had to feel, confound the old Recorder.

By paying up my costs and fines they freed me from the locker,
And then I started for the mines, I got a pick and rocker.
I went to work in an untouched place, I'm sure I meant no blame, sir,
But a white man struck me in the face and told me to leave his claim, sir.

'Twas then I packed my tools away and set up in a new place,
But there they would not let me stay, they did not like the *cue* race.
And then I knew not what to do, I could not get employ,
The Know Nothings would bid me go, 'twas *tu nah mug ahoy.*

I started then for Weaverville where Chinamen were thriving,
But found our China agents there in ancient feuds were driving.
So I pitched into politics, but with the weaker party,
The Cantons with their clubs and bricks did drub us out right hearty.

I started for Yreka then, I thought that I would stay there,
But found for even Chinamen the diggings would not pay there.
So I set up a washing shop, but how extremely funny,
The miners all had dirty clothes, but not a cent of money.

I met a big stout Indian once, he stopped me on the trail, sir,
He drew an awful scalping knife and I trembled for my tail, sir.
He caught me by the hair, it's true, in a manner quite uncivil,
But when he saw my awful cue, he thought I was the devil.

Oh, now my friends I'm going away from this infernal place, sir,
The balance of my days I'll spend with the celestial race, sir.
I'll go to raising rice and tea, I'll be a heathen ever,
For Christians all have treated me as men should be used never.

Despite these difficulties, California's Chinese population continued to increase. By the 1860s, recognizing their value as workers, California's "Big Four" (Collis Huntington, Mark Hopkins, Leland Stanford and Charles Crocker) employed ten thousand Chinese men to build the Central Pacific Railroad.

The Famine Song

During the fifty years between 1790 and 1840, fewer than one million immigrants came to the United States. During the next ten years, however, more than 1.7 million immigrants arrived, most of them from Germany and Ireland.

In September, 1845, a fungus growth infected the potato crop in Wexford and Waterford Counties in Ireland. The fungus caused potatoes, which the Irish called "praties," to rot in the ground. The blight spread throughout the country, and the crop failures resulted in a famine that lasted until 1849. In five years, Ireland's population dropped twenty-five per cent, from eight million to six million people. More than a million men, women and children died from starvation and disease.

Irish immigrants brought "The Famine Song" to the United States during the 1840s.

The Famine Song

Words and Music: Anonymous.

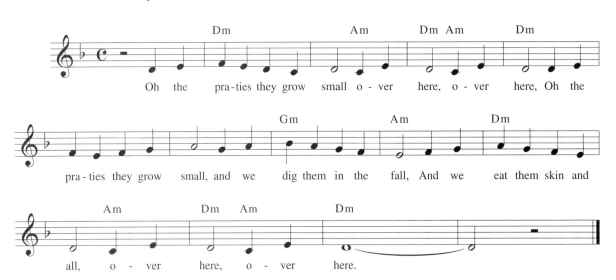

Oh the praties they grow small over here, over here,
Oh the praties they grow small, and we dig them in the fall,
And we eat them skin and all, over here, over here.

Oh we're down into the dust, over here, over here,
Oh we're down into the dust, and the Lord in whom we trust,
Shall repay us crumb for crust, over here, over here.

Oh we wish that we were geese, night and morn, night and morn,
Oh we wish that we were geese, and could live our lives in peace,
Till the hour of our release, eating corn, eating corn.

No Irish Need Apply

Of those who survived the famine, one million left Ireland to come to the United States. Thousands died on board ship from typhus, and ships carrying Irish immigrants became known as "coffin ships." The newly arrived Irish were set apart by their accents, their poverty and their customs. They were greeted with hostility and ridicule. Housing discrimination and job discrimination plagued the new Americans. Ads for jobs included the statement: "No Irish need apply."

"No Irish Need Apply" was published in New York by H. De Marsan Publisher during the Civil War. "Meagher's men" and "Corcoran's brigade" were New York Irish combat units in the Union Army. The famous comic singer Tony Pastor popularized the song.

The lure of American wages

No Irish Need Apply

Words and Music: J. F. Poole.

I'm a de - cent boy just land - ed from the town of Bai - ly - fad,

I want a sit - u - a - tion and I want it ver - y bad,

I have seen em - ploy - ment ad - ver - tised, "It's just the thing!" says

I, But the dirt - y spal - peen en - ded with "No I - rish need ap -

ply." "Whoo!" says I, "That is an in - sult, but to

get the place I'll try." So I went to see the black - guard with his no

I - rish need ap - ply. Some do think it a mis - for - tune to be

chris - tened Pat or Dan, But to me it is an hon - or to be

born an I - rish - man!

I'm a decent boy just landed from the town of Ballyfad,
I want a situation and I want it very bad,
I have seen employment advertised, "It's just the thing!" says I,
But the dirty *spalpeen* ended with "No Irish need apply."
"Whoo!" says I, "That is an insult, but to get the place I'll try."
So I went to see the blackguard with his no Irish need apply.

CHORUS
Some do think it a misfortune to be christened Pat or Dan,
But to me it is an honor to be born an Irishman!

Well I started out to find the place, I got there mighty soon,
I found the old chap seated, he was readin' the *Tribune*,
I told him what I came for, and he in a rage did fly,
"No!" he said, "You are a Paddy, and no Irish need apply."
Well I gets me dander risin' and I'd like to black his eye,
For to tell an Irish gentleman "No Irish need apply." CHORUS

Well I couldn't stand it longer, so a-hold of him I took,
And I gave him such a beating as he'd get at Donnybrook,
He hollered "*Milia murther*!" and to get away did try,
And he swore he'd never write again "No Irish need apply."
Well he made a big apology, I told him then, "Goodbye,"
Sayin', "When next you want a beating, write 'No Irish need apply.'" CHORUS

Sure I've heard that in America it always is the plan,
That an Irishman is just as good as any other man,
A home and hospitality they never will deny
The stranger near, or ever say, "No Irish need apply."
But some black sheep are in the flock, "A dirty lot!" say I
A dacint man will never write; "No Irish need apply." CHORUS

Sure Paddy's heart is in his hand, as all the world does know,
His praties and his whiskey he will share with friend or foe,
His door is always open to the stranger passing by,
He never thinks of saying, "None but Irish may apply."
And, in Columbia's history, his name is ranking high,
Then the Devil take the knave that writes "No Irish need apply." CHORUS

Ould Ireland on the battlefield a lasting fame has made,
We all have heard of Meagher's men, and Corcoran's brigade,
Though fools may flout and bigots rave, and fanatics they may cry,
Yet when they want good fighting men, the Irish may apply,
And when for freedom and the right they raise the battle cry,
Then the Rebel ranks begin to think, "No Irish need apply." CHORUS

Who Threw the Overalls in Mrs. Murphy's Chowder?

The American theater helped sustain the Irish stereotype. The stage Irishman was a bizarre character, dressed in knee breeches, who spoke with a brogue, using words like "smithereens," "coleen," "begorra," "bejabbers" and "Erin go bragh." He distilled his own whiskey and he loved to drink and fight.

Who Threw the Overalls in Mrs. Murphy's Chowder?

Words and Music: George L. Giefer.

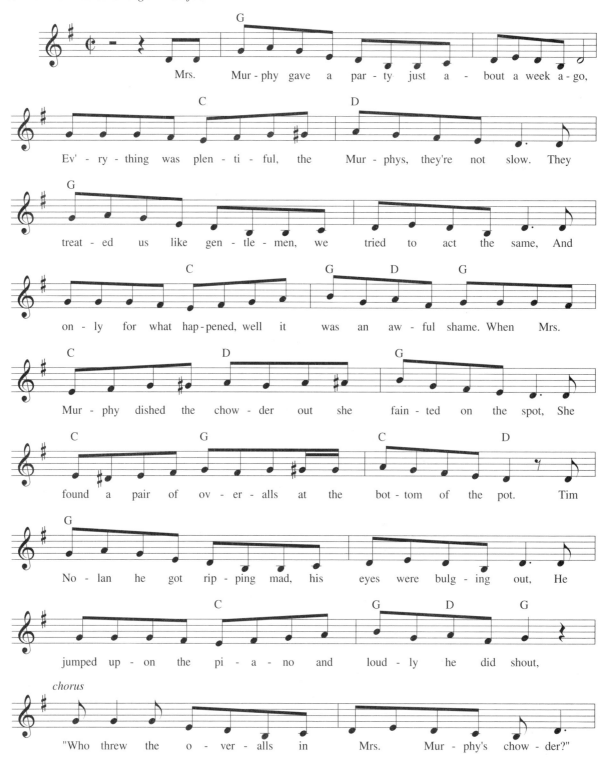

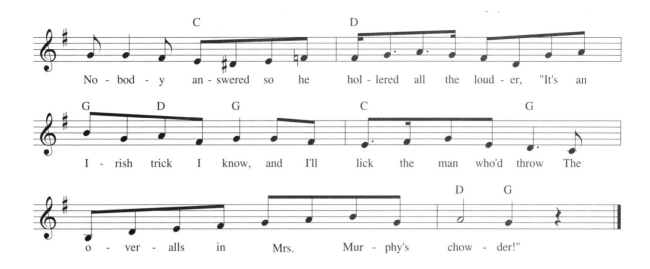

No - bod - y an - swered so he hol - lered all the loud - er, "It's an

I - rish trick I know, and I'll lick the man who'd throw The

o - ver - alls in Mrs. Mur - phy's chow - der!"

Mrs. Murphy gave a party just about a week ago,
Ev'rything was plentiful, the Murphys, they're not slow.
They treated us like gentlemen, we tried to act the same,
And only for what happened, well it was an awful shame.
When Mrs. Murphy dished the chowder out she fainted on the spot,
She found a pair of overalls at the bottom of the pot.
Tim Nolan he got ripping mad, his eyes were bulging out,
He jumped upon the piano and loudly he did shout,

CHORUS
"Who threw the overalls in Mrs. Murphy's chowder?"
Nobody answered so he hollered all the louder,
"It's an Irish trick I know, and I'll lick the man who'd throw
The overalls in Mrs. Murphy's chowder!"

They dragged the pants from out the soup and laid them on the floor,
Each man swore upon his life, he'd ne'er seen them before.
They were plastered up with mortar and were worn out at the knee,
They had their many ups and downs as we could plainly see.
And when Mrs. Murphy she came to she began to cry and pout,
She had them in the wash that day and forgot to take them out.
Tim Nolan, he excused himself for what he said that night,
So we put music to the words and sang with all our might. CHORUS

Irish stereotype

Mrs. Mulligan (*to Mr. Mulligan, cutting up old railroad ties for firewood*): "Ah, an' sure it's a foine sthroke yez have! An' it's the makin' of an illigint golf player yer have in yez!"

Lather 'n' Shave 'Em

Most of the Irish immigrants settled in America's larger cities, finding employment as unskilled workers. Large Irish communities populated New York and Boston, others moved west to Chicago and other major cities across the continent. A sizeable Irish community existed in California during the gold rush. Many worked on the railroads, and Irish-Americans and Irish immigrants fought on both sides of the Civil War.

Irish plays became as popular as minstrel shows. Some of the minstrel songs became stage-Irish songs. For example, "The Grand Old Colored Gentleman" became "The Grand Old Irish Gentleman."

In the popular 19th century stage-Irish song "Lather 'n' Shave 'Em," the Irishman asks the barber for a shave on credit, and gets more than he bargained for. Keith McNeil's grandfather, Will Oakley, a California cattle rancher, sang this version in the early 1900s.

Lather 'n' Shave 'Em

Words and Music: Anonymous.

A barber he opened a nice little shop, And he got him a mug and a brush and a strop, And he got him a ra-zor full of notch-es and rust To shave them poor dev-ils who came there for trust. With his

Lath-er 'n' shave 'em, lath-er 'n' shave 'em, Lath-er 'n' shave 'em, friz-zle um bum.

A barber he opened a nice little shop,
And he got him a mug and a brush and a strop,
And he got him a razor full of notches and rust
To shave them poor devils who came there for trust. With his

CHORUS
Lather 'n' shave 'em, lather 'n' shave 'em,
Lather 'n' shave 'em, frizzle um bum.

It happened that an Irishman was passin' that way,
Whose beard had been growin' for many a day.
He entered the shop and he said with a nod,
"Will you trust me a shave for the pure love of God?" With your CHORUS

The barber said, "Sure and I'll shave you for trust."
And he got out his razor full of notches and rust.
As he scraped and he pulled Paddy started to yell,
But he held him down tight and he shaved him fair well. With his CHORUS

Well Paddy he jumped out onto the floor,
And Paddy he bolted right out of the door,
Sayin', "You can lather and shave all your friends till you're sick,
But bejabbers I'd rather be shaved with a brick!" Than your CHORUS

The Night That Paddy Murphy Died

Irish wakes have been the subject of countless songs and stories. For example, Irish author James Joyce's classic book *Finnegan's Wake* used the not-so-dead Finnegan to represent Ireland. The American song "Pat Malone's Wake" has Pat playing dead to collect the insurance. "The Night That Paddy Murphy Died" is another American favorite.

The Night That Paddy Murphy Died

Words and Music: Anonymous.

The night that Pad-dy Mur-phy died I nev-er will for-get, The I-rish all got stink-in' drunk and some ain't so-ber yet, The first thing that they did that night that filled me heart with fear, They took the ice right off the corpse and put it on the beer! *chorus* That's how we showed our re-spect for Pad-dy Mur-phy, That's how we showed our hon-or and our pride, oh Lord-y, That's how we showed our re-spect for Pad-dy Mur-phy, The night that Pad-dy died.

The night that Paddy Murphy died I never will forget,
The Irish all got stinkin' drunk and some ain't sober yet,
The first thing that they did that night that filled me heart with fear,
They took the ice right off the corpse and put it on the beer!

CHORUS
That's how we showed our respect for Paddy Murphy,
That's how we showed our honor and our pride, oh Lordy,
That's how we showed our respect for Paddy Murphy,
The night that Paddy died.

The Bold Fenian Men

Irish nationalism came to America, too. The new Irish-Americans formed a secret brotherhood dedicated to Irish independence. They called themselves "Fenians" after the legendary Irish hero Finn McCool. The Fenians, or Irish Republican Brotherhood (I.R.B.), was organized in 1858 in Ireland and in New York under the leadership of James Stephens and John O'Mahoney. They believed that force was the way to independence. In Ireland, the Fenian rising of 1867 failed. In England, the Fenian attempt to capture Chester Castle also failed, as did their raids in Canada (by Irish-American Fenians) in the late 1860s.

Patrick Byrne, blind harper, mid-19th century

The Bold Fenian Men

Words: Peader Kearney. Music: Anonymous.

'Twas down by the glen-side I met an old wom-an,
A-pluck-in' young net-tles, nor saw I was com-in',
I lis-tened a while to the song she was hum-min',
"Glo-ry oh, glo-ry oh, to the bold Fe-nian men."

'Twas down by the glen-side I met an old woman,
A-pluckin' young nettles, nor saw I was comin',
I listened a while to the song she was hummin',
"Glory oh, glory oh, to the bold Fenian men."

"'Tis fifty long years since I saw the moon beaming,
And strong manly forms and their eyes with hope gleaming,
I see them again, sure through all my days dreaming,
Glory oh, glory oh, to the bold Fenian men."

"When I was a colleen their marching and drilling,
Awoke by the glen-side sounds awesome and thrilling,
They loved dear old Ireland, and to die they were willing,
Glory oh, glory oh, to the bold Fenian men."

"Some died by the glen-side, some died amid strangers,
And wise men have told us their cause was a failure,
But they stood by old Ireland, and they never feared danger,
Glory oh, glory oh, to the bold Fenian men."

I passed on my way, God be praised that I met her,
Be life long or short, I will never forget her,
There may be brave men, but there'll never be better,
Glory oh, glory oh, to the bold Fenian men.

Die Gedanken Sind Frei

In contrast to the Irish, many of the mid-19th century German immigrants were intellectuals, university graduates and others of high economic and social standing. After Napoleon's defeat in Europe, the peace conference in Vienna in 1814-15 failed to unify the German Empire. Instead, a bund, or confederation of German states, was organized with each state having its own constitution, laws, taxes, flag and army. In response, German nationalists organized a revolutionary movement to create a unified and democratic Germany. After the revolution of 1848-49 failed, and the bund was restored, thousands of German liberals migrated to America in search of freedom.

They brought with them a traditional German students' song called "Die Gedanken Sind Frei" (The Thoughts Are Free). Folk music scholar Arthur Kevess, in his book *German Folk Songs*, says the song first appeared in Silesian and Hessian broadsides between 1780 and 1820, and that it was first published as a song in Switzerland between 1810 and 1820. Some scholars believe that the song originated much earlier, during the Peasant's War of 1542. It is still sung in Germany and the United States.

The words say:

Thoughts are free! Who could guess them? They rush by like shadows in the night. No one knows them, no hunter can shoot them. Yes, thoughts are free. I keep them to myself. No one can deny my wishes and desires. You can lock me in the darkest dungeon, but my thoughts will burst through the barriers and walls. Thoughts are free!

German liberals fighting government troops in Germany 1848

Die Gedanken Sind Frei

Words and Music: Anonymous.

Die Ge - dan - ken sind frei, wer kann sie er -
ra - ten? Sie flie - hen vor - bei wie nächt - li - che
Schat - ten. Kein Mensch kann sie wis - sen, kein Jä - ger er -
schie - ssen, Es blei - bet da - bei: Die Ge - dan - ken sind frei!

Die Gedanken sind frei, wer kann sie erraten?
Sie fliehen vorbei wie nächtliche Schatten.
Kein Mensch kann sie wissen, kein Jäger erschiessen,
Es bleibet dabei: Die Gedanken sind frei!

Ich denke, was ich will und was mich beglücket.
Doch alles in der Still, und wie es sich schicket.
Mein Wunsch und Begehren kann niemand verwehren,
Es bleibet dabei: Die Gedanken sind frei!

Und sperrt man mich ein im finsteren Kerker,
Das alles sind rein vergebliche Werke,
Dann meine Gedanken zerreissen die Schranken
Und Mauern entzwei: Die Gedanken sind frei!

O Tannenbaum

German immigrants in the mid-nineteenth century settled throughout the United States. German brewers settled in Milwaukee. In Kansas, German-Russian Mennonite farmers brought the Turkey Red winter wheat, while German stonecutters quarried the limestone that lay just beneath the surface, using it to build houses, barns, churches and fence posts. German farmers settled communities like Fredricksburg on the Texas plains, and others came to California to find gold.

German immigrants were influential in the way Americans celebrate Christmas. In early America the Dutch in New York celebrated with ice-skating, drinking, lighting the yule log and giving gifts to children in memory of St. Nicholas.

Puritans in Massachusetts didn't celebrate Christmas at all, and in 1659 levied a fine of five shillings on anyone who observed the holiday. The English in Virginia lighted the yule log, feasted, drank hot toddies and held a fox hunt. It was the 19th century Germans who brought the custom of celebrating Christmas as a church-oriented festival.

These Germans also brought their Christmas trees, and the story that all living things, including the trees, went to visit the Christ child. The fir was embarrassed because it had no fruit to offer, so the stars took pity and settled in the fir tree, to the delight of the baby Jesus. The fir tree remains to this day the symbolic tree of Christmas. Germans also brought their lovely Christmas songs, including "O Tannenbaum."

O Tannenbaum

Words and Music: Anonymous.

O Tan - nen - baum, O Tan - nen - baum, Wie treu sind dei - ne Blä - ter! O Tan - nen - baum, O Tan - nen - baum, Wie treu sind dei - ne Blä - ter! Du grünst nicht nur zur Som - mer - zeit, Nein auch im Win - ter, wenn es schneit. O Tan - nen - baum, O Tan-nen-baum, Wie treu sind dei-ne Blä - ter!

O Tannenbaum, O Tannenbaum,
Wie treu sind deine Bläter!
O Tannenbaum, O Tannenbaum,
Wie treu sind deine Bläter!
Du grünst nicht nur zur Sommerzeit,
Nein auch im Winter, wenn es schneit.
O Tannenbaum, O Tannenbaum,
Wie treu sind deine Bläter!

American version:

Oh Christmas tree, oh Christmas tree,
How lovely are your branches.
Oh Christmas tree, oh Christmas tree,
How lovely are your branches.
They're green when summer days are bright,
They're green when winter snow is white,
Oh Christmas tree, oh Christmas tree,
How lovely are your branches.

Du, Du, Liegst Mir im Herzen

Many songs brought to America by German immigrants have become American standards, still sung in German. These include "Ach, Du Lieber Augustin," "Die Lorelei," "Schnitzelbank" and "Du, Du, Liegst Mir Im Herzen."

The words to "Du, Du, Liegst Mir im Herzen" say:

You rest in my heart. You rest in my mind. You cause me much pain, you don't realize how good I am for you. Yes, yes, yes, yes, you don't realize how good I am for you. So the way I love you, love me too. These tender thoughts I feel only for you. But can I trust you with your free thinking? You can rely on me, you know how good I am for you. Yes, you know how good I am for you. And when we are apart and my image appears to you, I hope that love will join us together, yes, that love will join us together!

Du, Du, Liegst Mir im Herzen

Words and Music: Anonymous.

Du, du liegst mir im Herzen,
Du, du liegst mir im Sinn,
Du, du machst mir viel Schmerzen,
Weisst nicht wie gut ich dir bin.
Ja, ja, ja, ja,
Weisst nicht wie gut ich dir bin.

So, so wie ich dich liebe,
So, so liebe auch mich!
Die, die zärtlichsten Triebe
Fühl ich allein nur für dich.
Ja, ja, ja, ja,
Fühl ich allein nur für dich.

Doch, doch darf ich dir trauen,
Dir, dir mit leichtem Sinn?
Du, du darfst auf mich bauen,
Weisst ja, wie gut ich dir bin!
Ja, ja, ja, ja,
Weisst ja, wie gut ich dir bin!

Und, und wenn in der Ferne,
Dir, dir mein Bild erscheint,
Dann, dann wünscht ich so gerne,
Dass uns die Liebe vereint!
Ja, ja, ja, ja,
Dass uns die Liebe vereint!

German band

During the 1840s and 1850s storm clouds were gathering
for an event which would temporarily halt the huge influx of
immigrants and the great migration westward. Lines were
being drawn geographically, economically, ideologically and
politically which would plunge the nation into civil war.

Sources for and about Moving West Songs:

Best, Dick and Beth. *Song Fest*. Crown Publishers, Inc., 1948.

Botkin, B. A. *A Treasury of Western Folklore*. New York: Crown Publishers, Inc., 1951.

Cheney, Thomas E. *Mormon Songs From the Rocky Mountains*. Salt Lake City: University of Utah Press, 1981.

Doerflinger, William Main. *Songs of the Sailor and Lumberman*. New York: The Macmillan Company, 1972.

Dolph, Edward Arthur. *"Sound Off!" Soldier Songs*. Cosmopolitan Book Corporation, 1929.

Drew, Benjamin. *The Narratives of Fugitive Slaves in Canada*. Cleveland, Ohio: John P. Jewett and Company, 1856. Facsimile edition published by Coles Publishing Company, Toronto, 1972.

Dwyer, Richard A., Richard E. Lingenfelter and David Cohen. *Songs of the Gold Rush*. Berkeley and Los Angeles: University of California Press, 1965.

Greenway, John. *American Folksongs of Protest*. University of Pennsylvania Press, 1953.

Howard, John Tasker. *Stephen Foster, America's Troubadour*. New York: Thomas Y. Crowell Company, 1934.

Jackson, George Pullen. *White Spirituals in the Southern Uplands*. North Carolina: University of North Carolina Press, Chapel Hill., 1933. Facsimile edition published by Dover Publications, Inc., New York, 1965.

Kennedy, Peter. *Folksongs of Britain and Ireland*. London, New York, Sydney, Cologne: Oak Publications, 1984.

Kevess, Arthur. *German Folk Songs*. New York: Oak Publications, 1968.

Lloyd, Ruth and Norman Lloyd. *The American Heritage Songbook*. New York, American Heritage Publishing Co., Inc., 1969.

Lingenfelter, Richard E., Richard A. Dwyer and David Cohen. *Songs of the American West*. Berkeley and Los Angeles: University of California Press, 1968.

Lomax, Alan. *The Folk Songs of North America*. Garden City, New York: Doubleday & Company, 1960.

Lomax, John A. and Alan Lomax. *American Ballads and Folk Songs*. New York: The Macmillan Company, 1934.

Lummis, Charles F. *Spanish Songs of Old California*. Los Angeles: Chas. F. Lummis, 1925.

Marsh, J. B. T. *The Story of the Jubilee Singers*. Boston: Houghton, Osgood and Company, 1880.

O'Neill, Capt. Francis. *Irish Minstrels and Musicians*. Chicago: The Regan Printing House, 1913.

Patterson, Peter Blood. *Rise Up Singing*. Bethlehem, Pennsylvania: Sing Out Corporation, 1988.

Sandburg, Carl. *The American Songbag*. New York: Harcourt, Brace & Company, 1927.

Scott, John Anthony. *The Ballad of America: The History of the United States in Song and Story*. New York, Toronto, London: Bantam Pathfinder Editions, 1966.

Shull, Paul. *Music in the West*. Manhattan, Kansas: Sunflower University Press, 1983.

Stone, John A. *Put's Original California Songster*. 1855.

Wade, J. *Christy's Minstrels' New Songs, With Choruses in Vocal Score, Symphonies and Pianoforte Accompaniments. Volumes 1, 2, and 3*. London, "Musical Bouquet" Office, 192 High Holborn; J. Allen, 20 Warwick Lane, Paternoster Row, 1861.

White, B. F. *"Original Sacred Harp" Denson revision*. Cullman, Alabama: Sacred Harp Publishing Company, Inc., 1960.

Williams, William H. A. *'Twas Only an Irishman's Dream: The Image of Ireland and the Irish in American Popular Song Lyrics, 1800-1920*. Urbana and Chicago: University of Illinois Press, 1996.

Picture Credits:

Index of Songs:

Acknowledgements:

Our thanks to Darrin Schuck for assistance on musical notation, to Joe Rael and Sonia Camacho for Spanish translations, to Hannes Linke and Jennifer McNeil Miller for German translations, to Ted Moews for historical and artistic assistance, to Mary McNeil Cheever, Connie McNeil and Sarah McNeil for content suggestions and proofreading, to Judith Auth for access to the historical and pictorial resources at the Riverside Public Library, to Jennifer Cutting and Todd Harvey at The Library of Congress for their help in finding authors, publishers and publication dates of songs, to Ellen Harding at the California State Library for picture permissions, to John Garrett Short for design work and layout, and to all friends, students, teachers and family who have shared their music with us over the past 50 years.